LIANELLA MAY

YUMMY FOOD COLORING BOOK

25 TOTALLY FRAMEABLE COLORING PAGES

Artworks copyright © 2018 Lianella May. All rights reserved.

No part of this book may be reproduced or transmitted in any form or by any means, electronic and mechanical, including photocopying, recording or by any information storage and retrieval system, without written permission from the publisher.

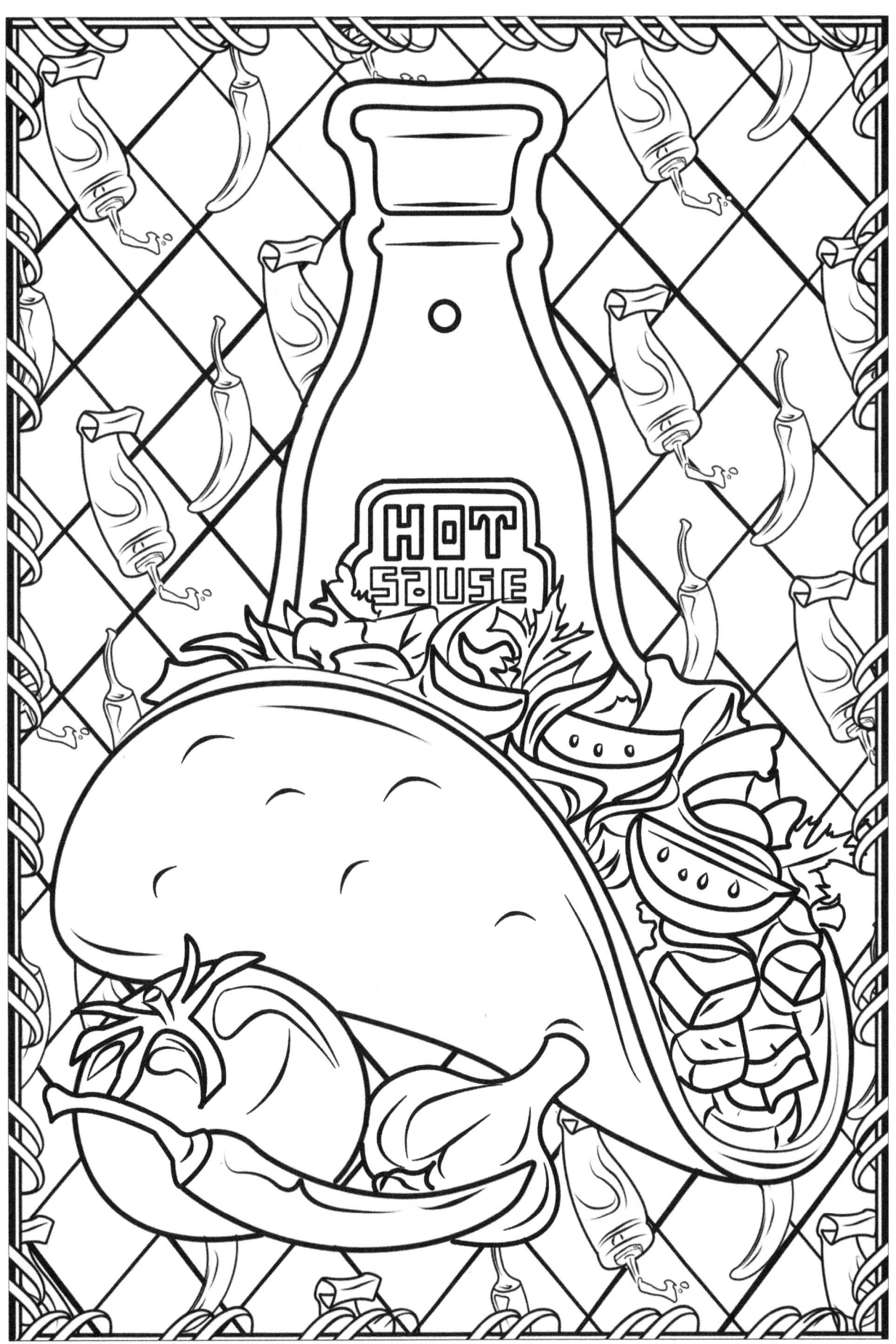

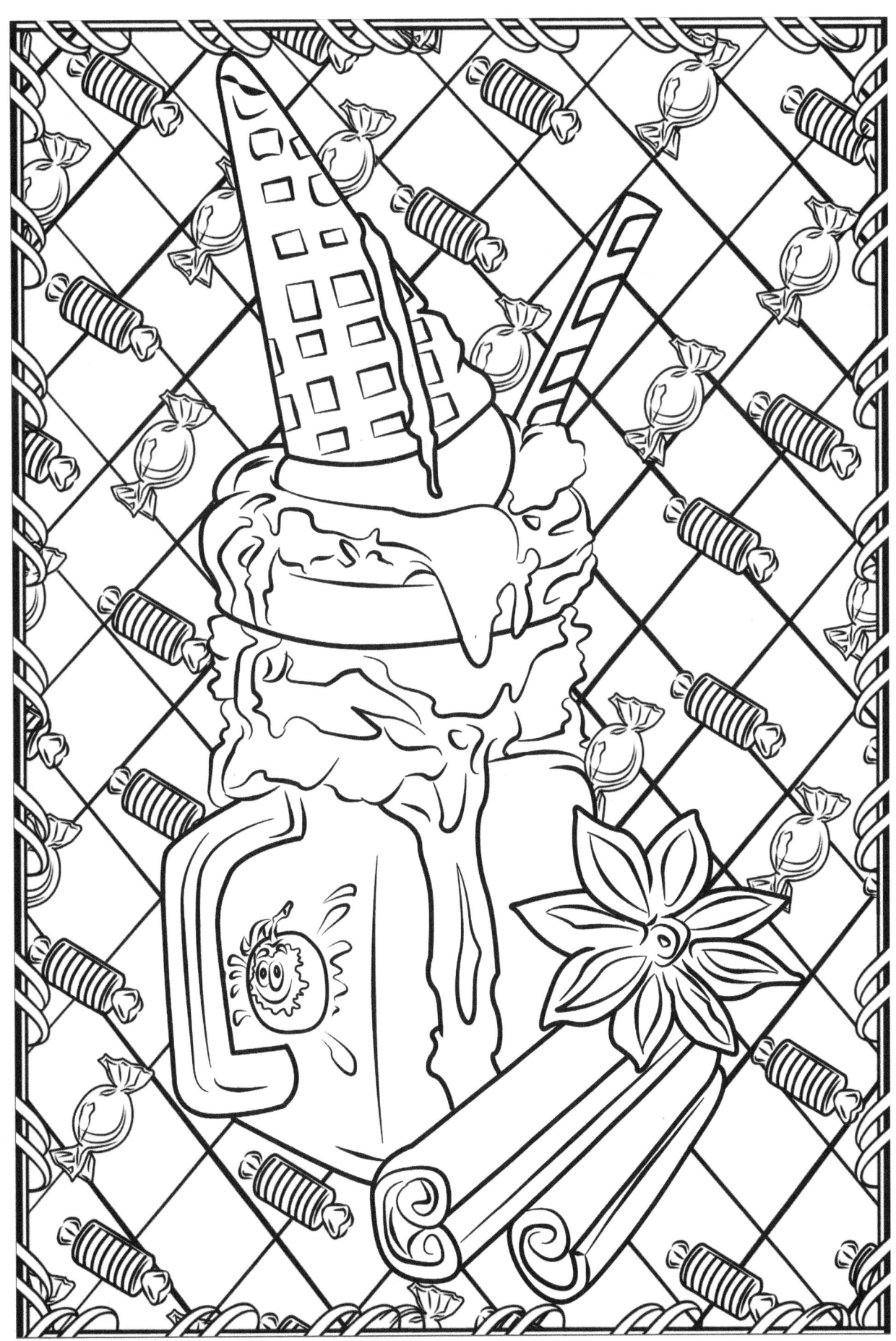

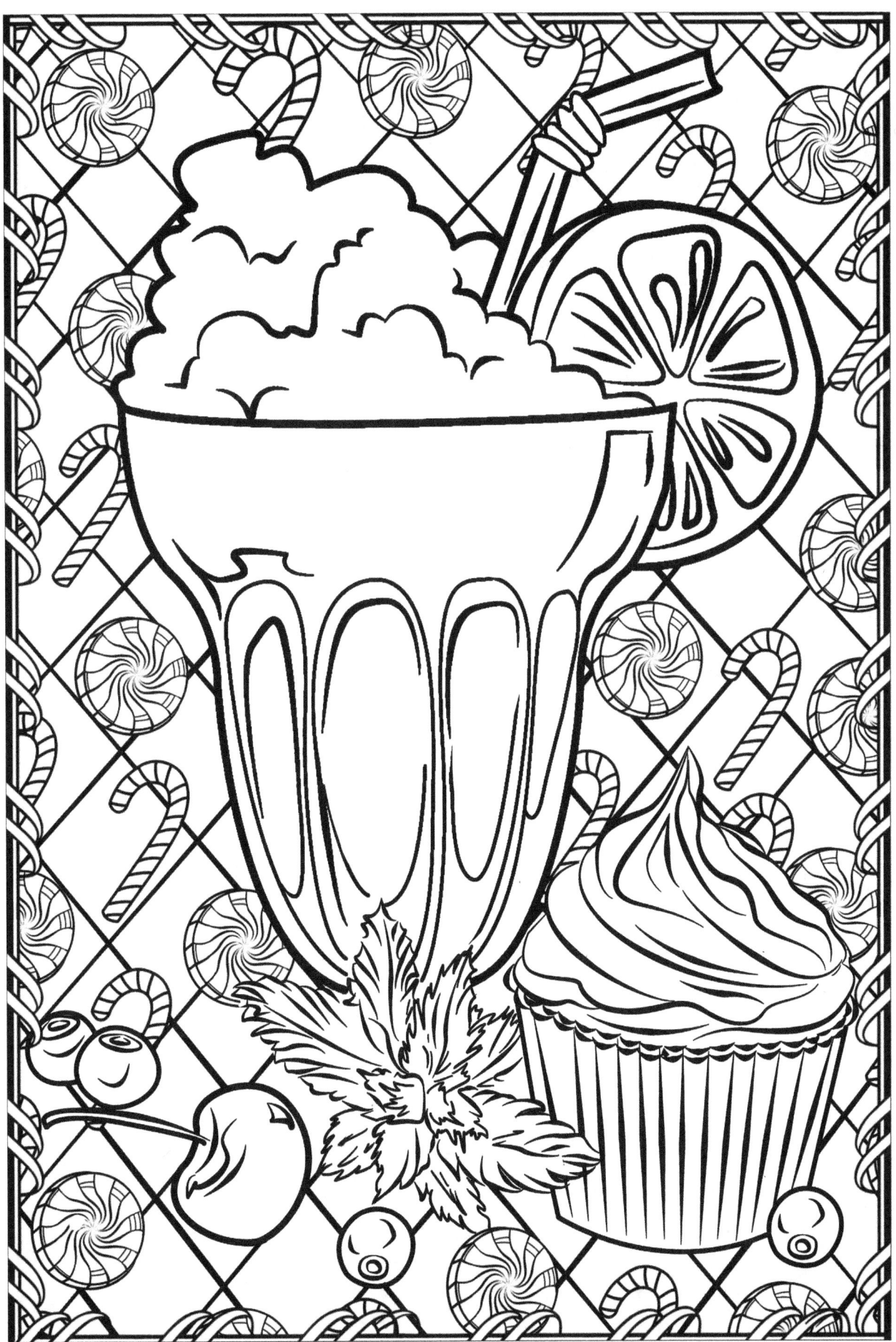

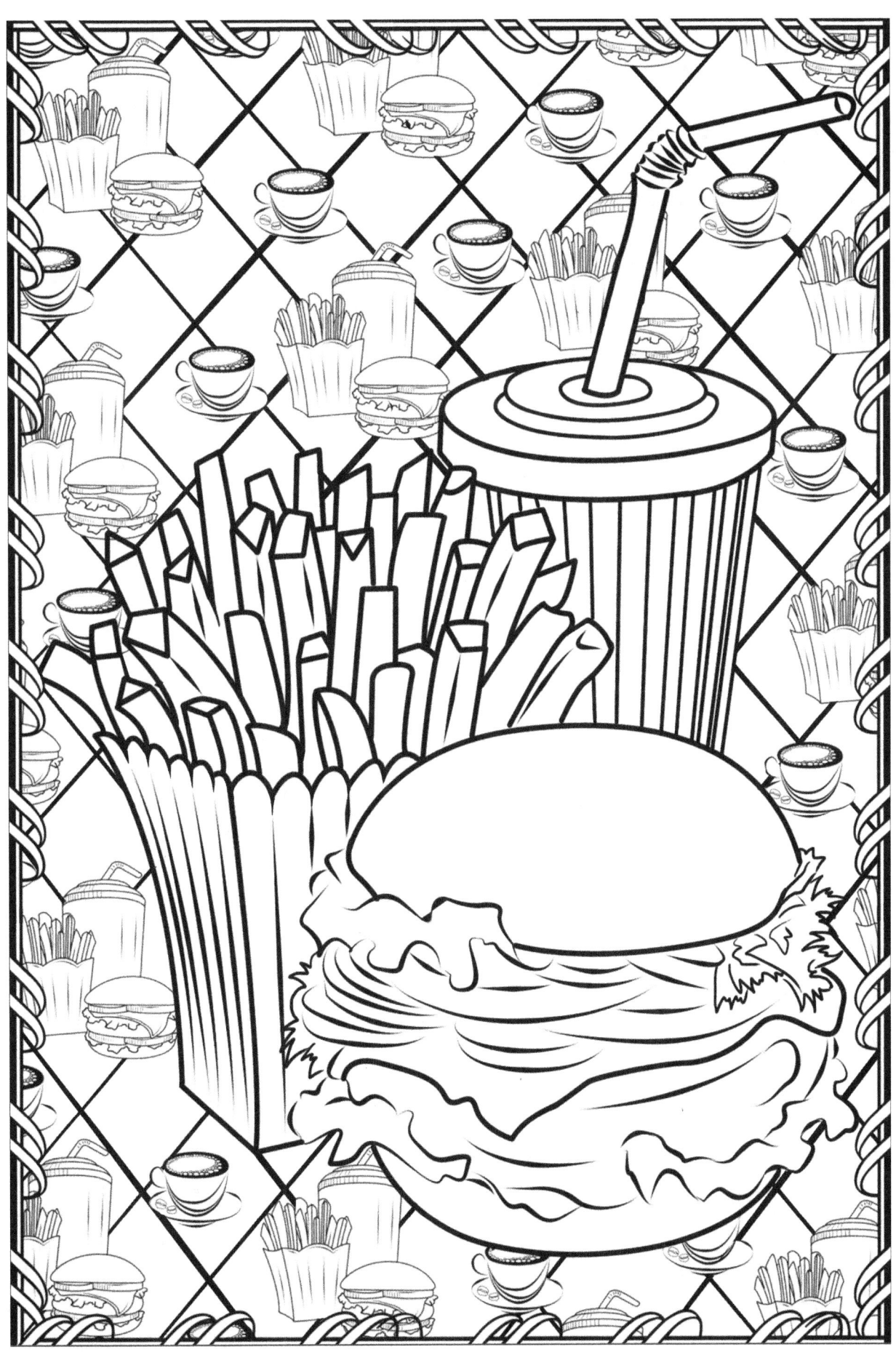

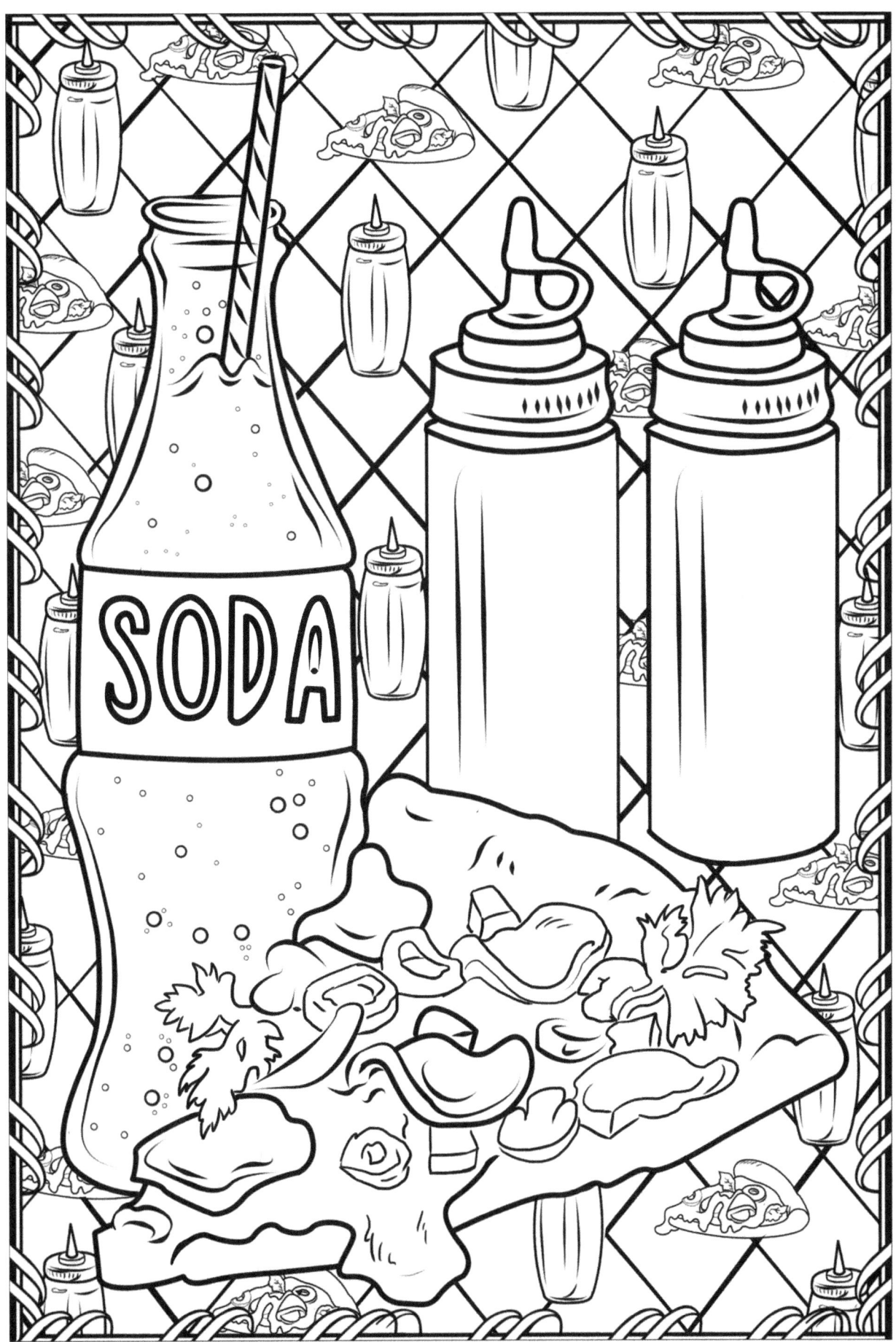

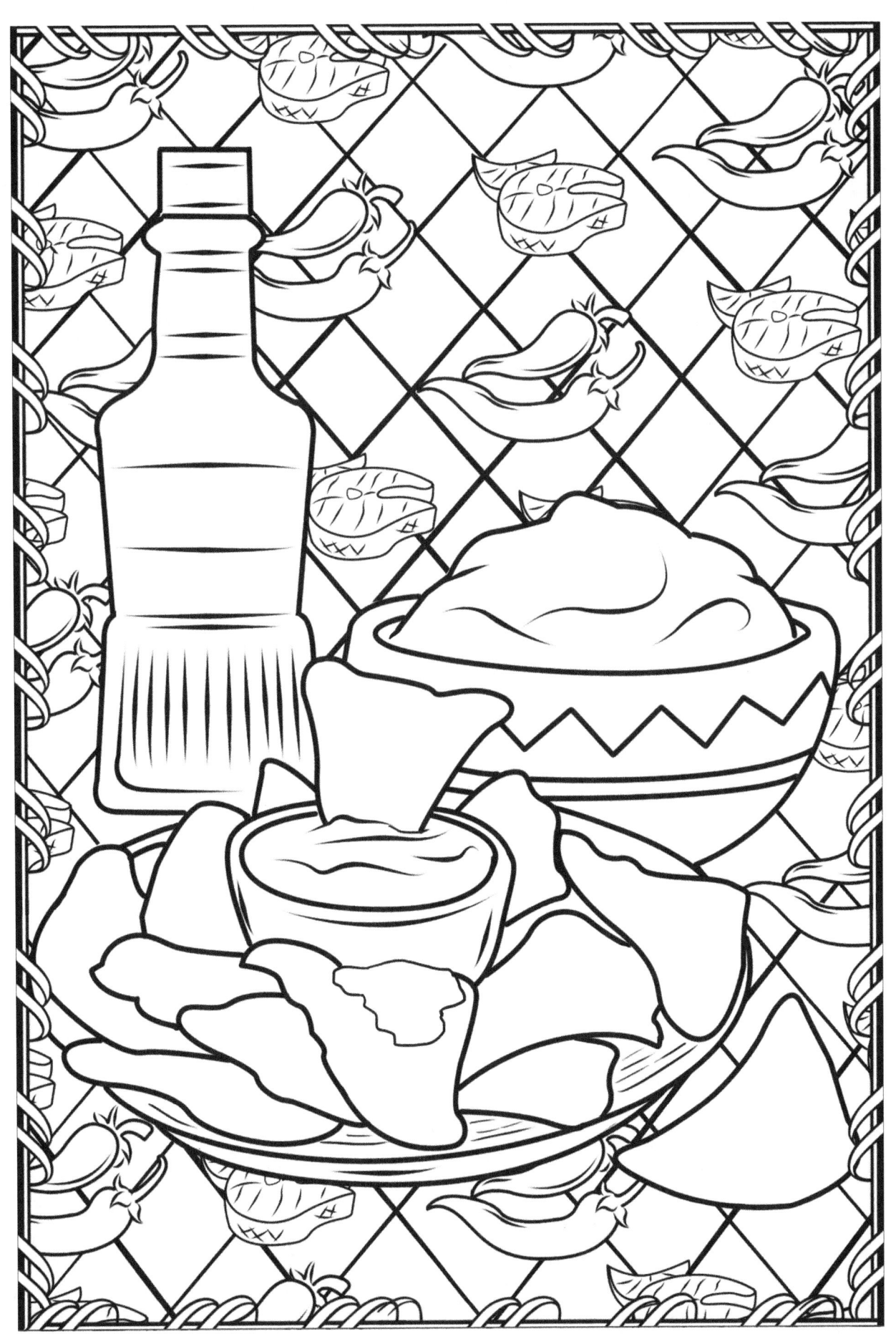

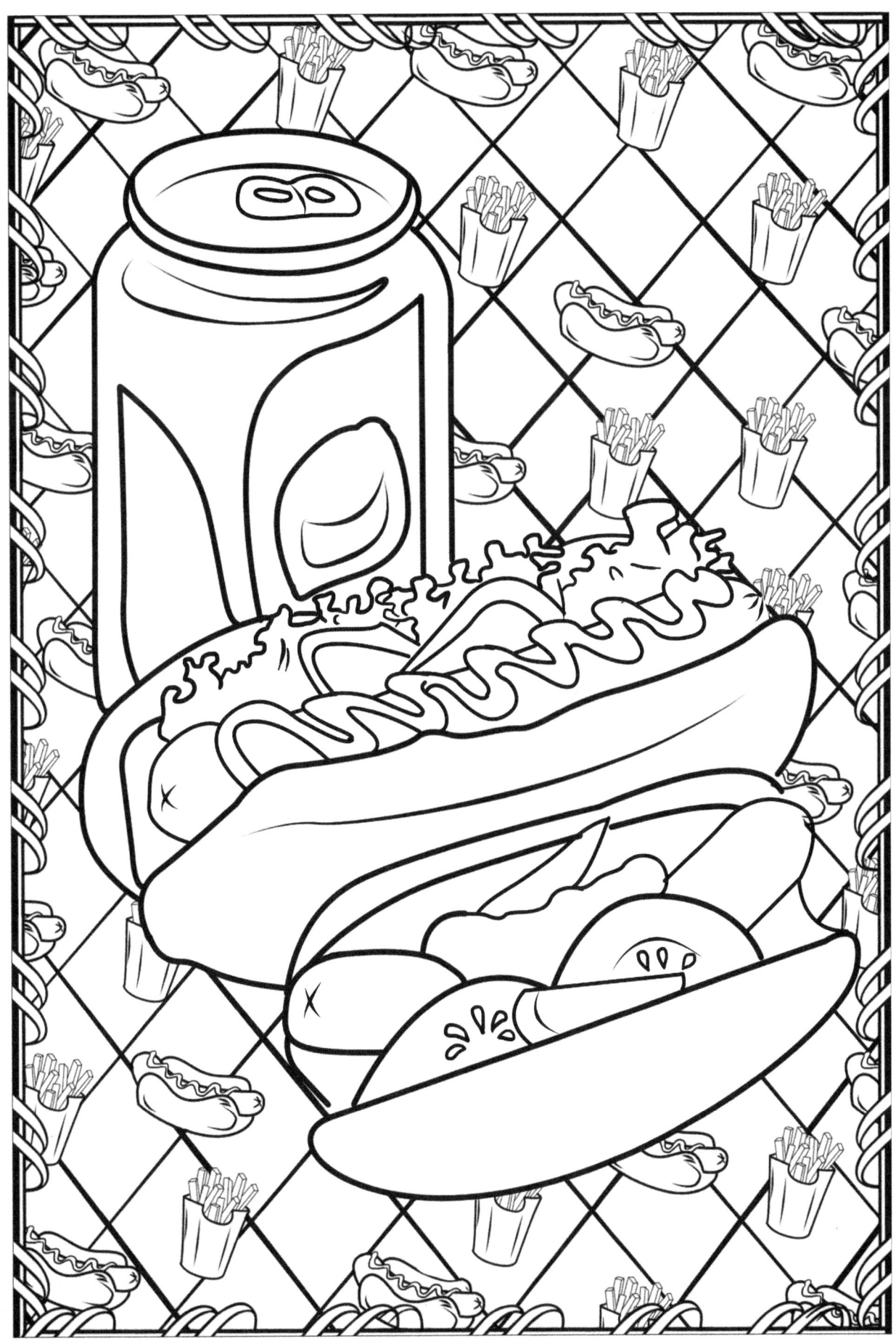

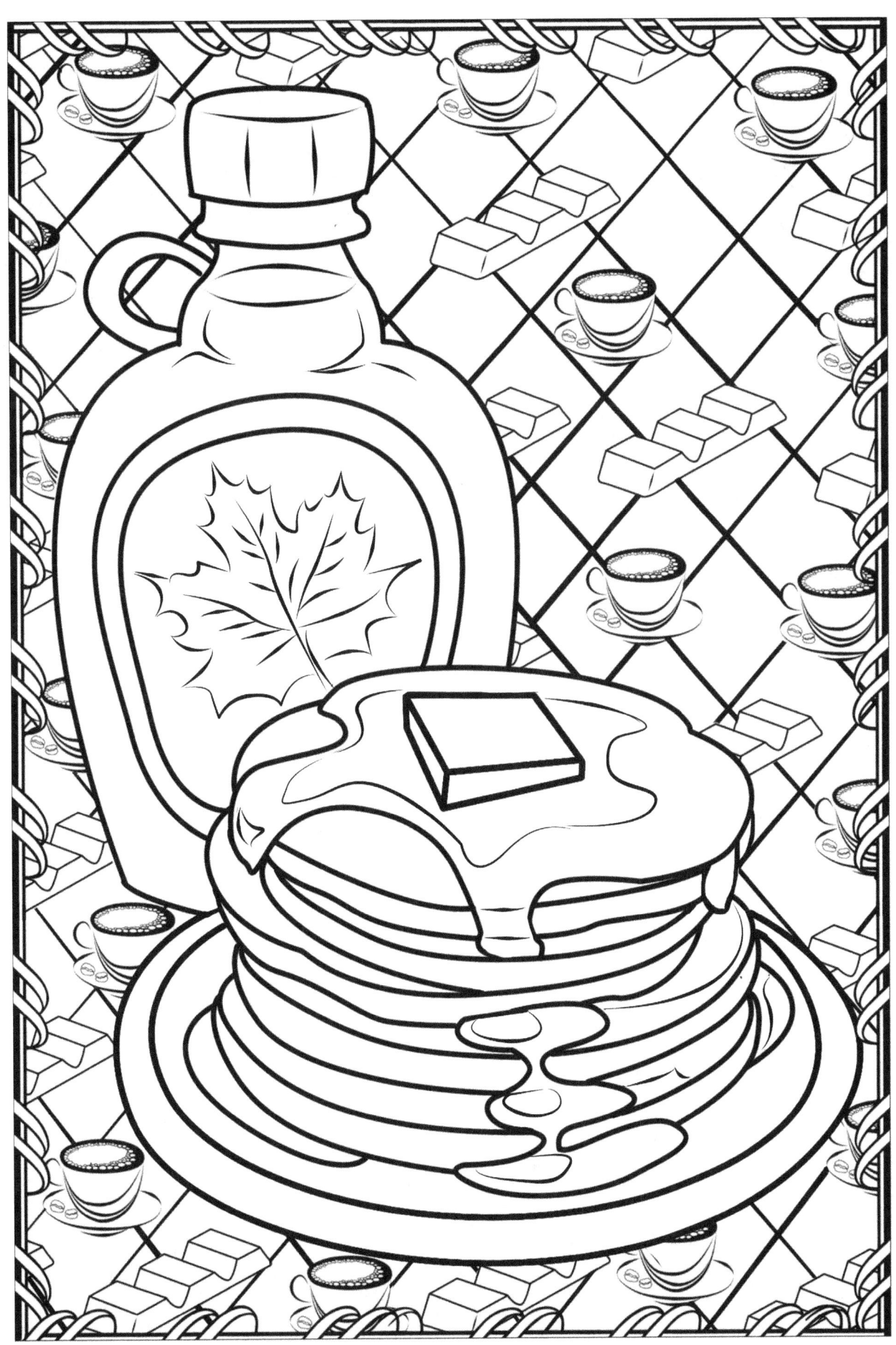

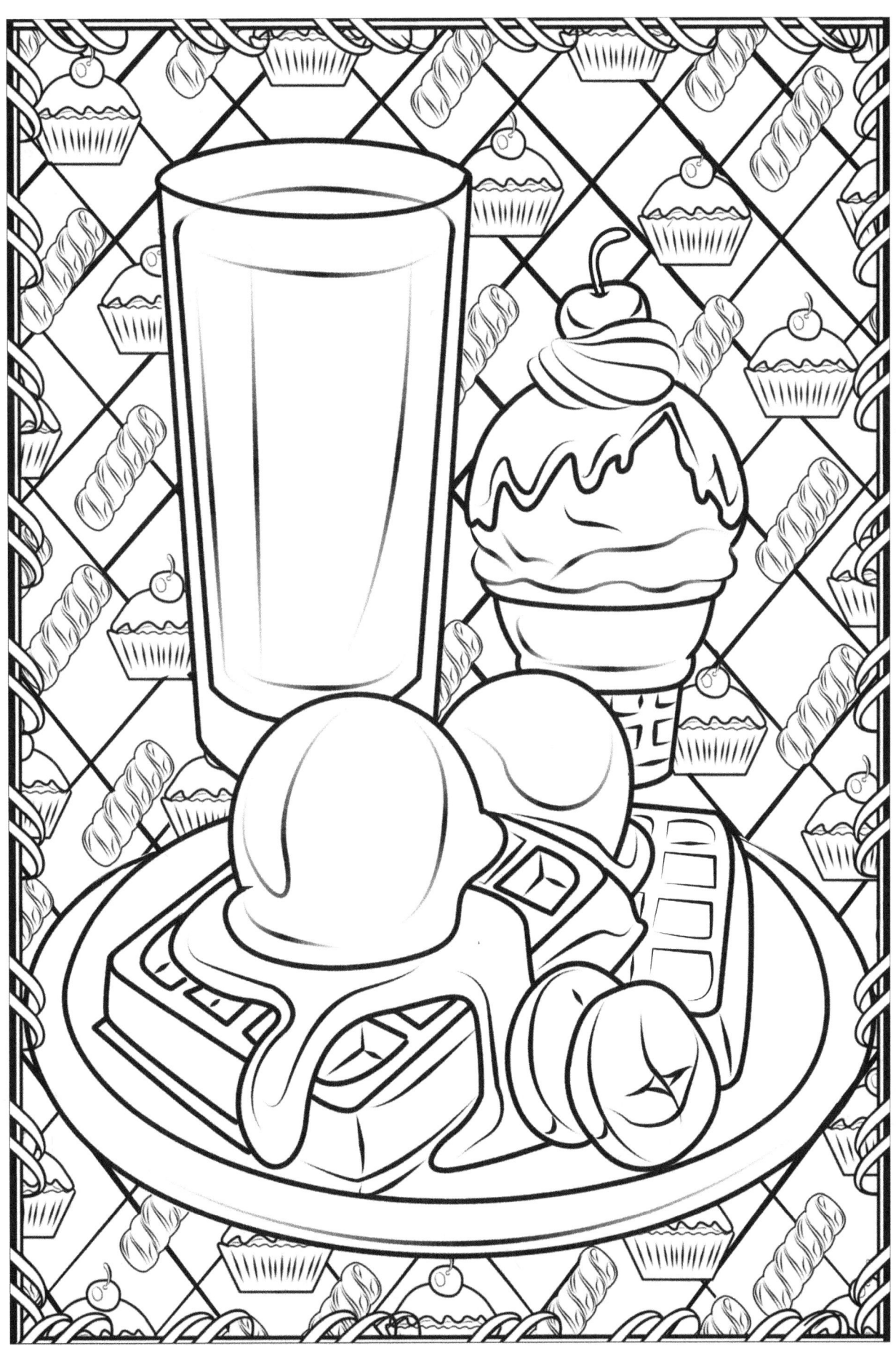

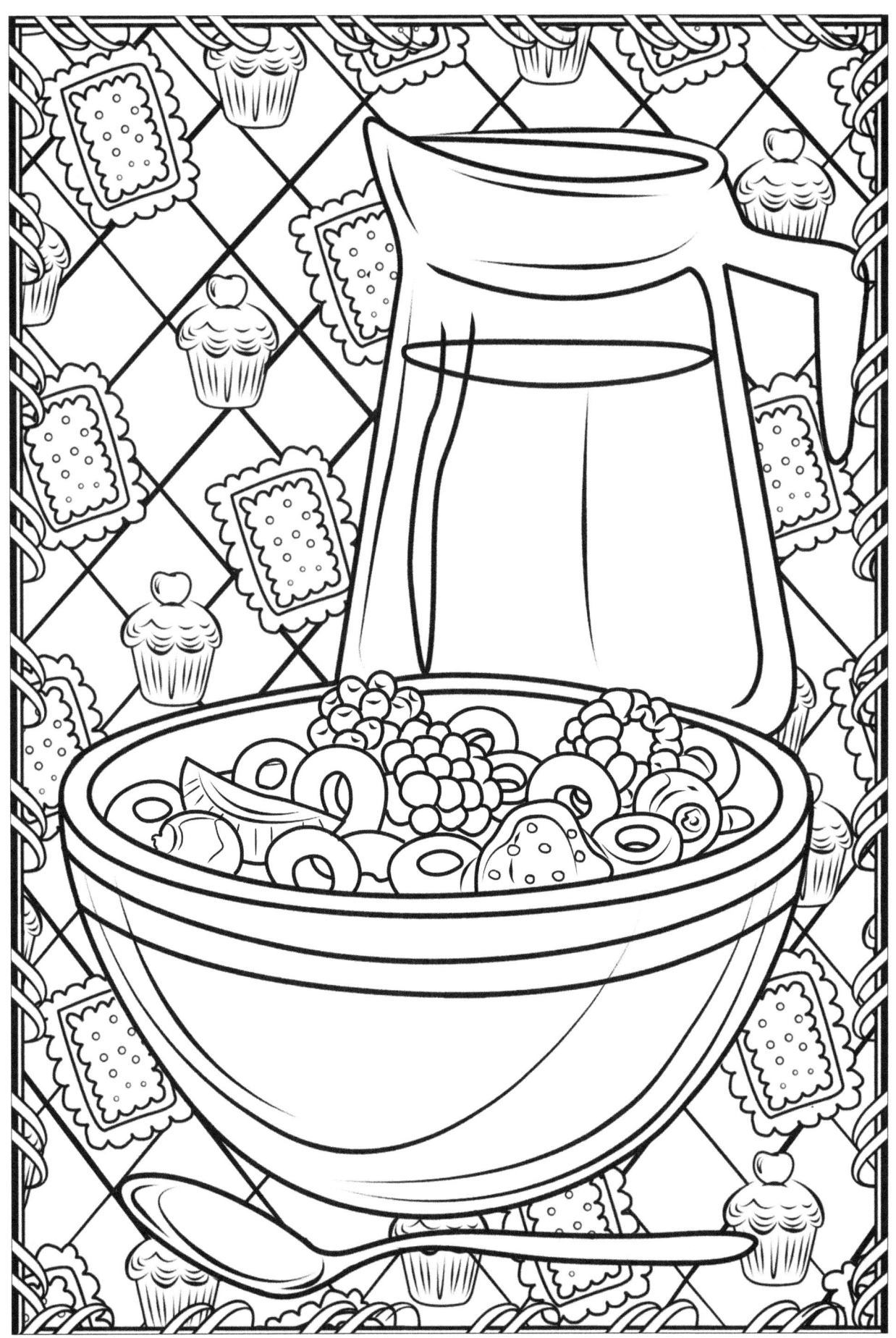

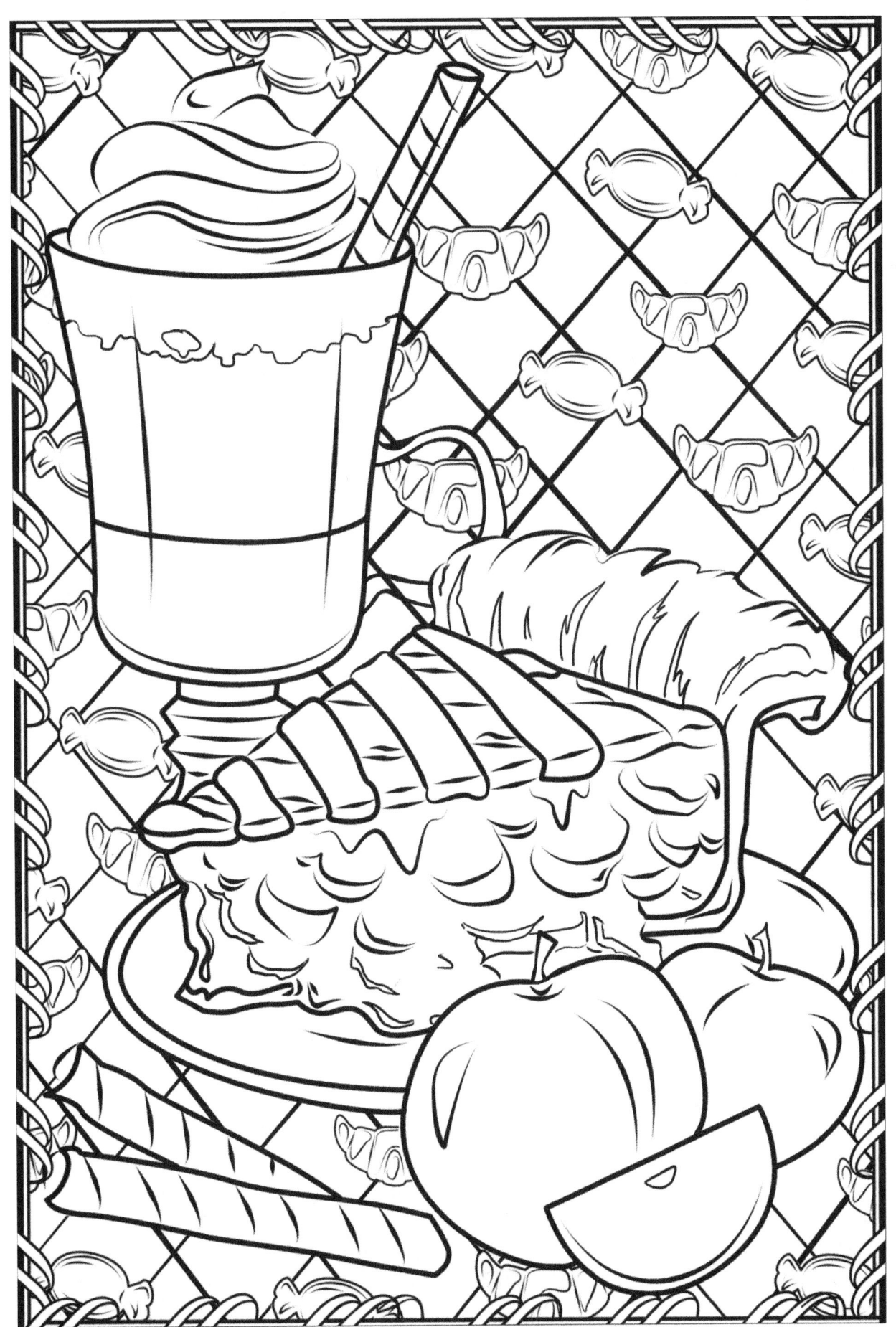

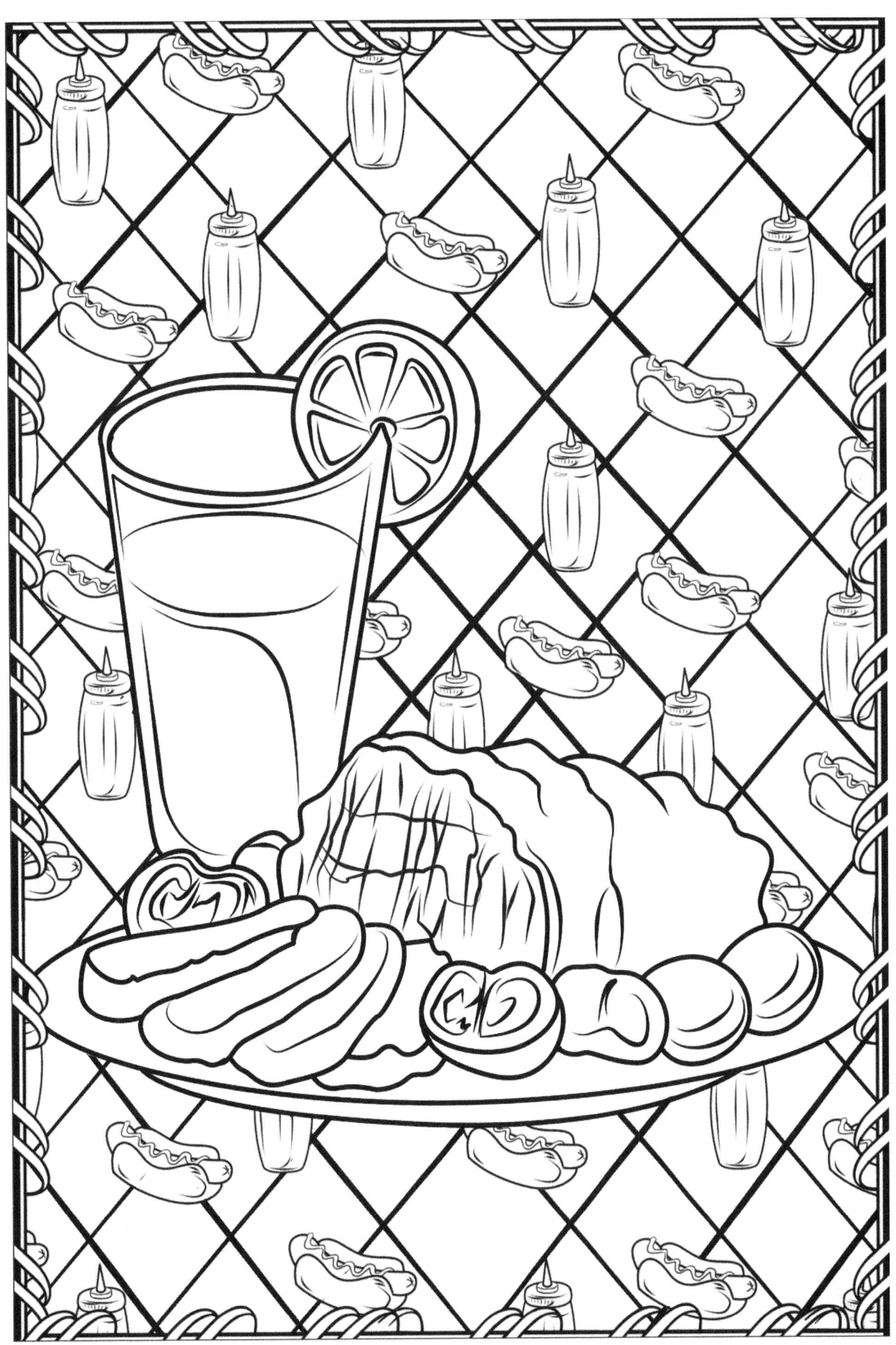

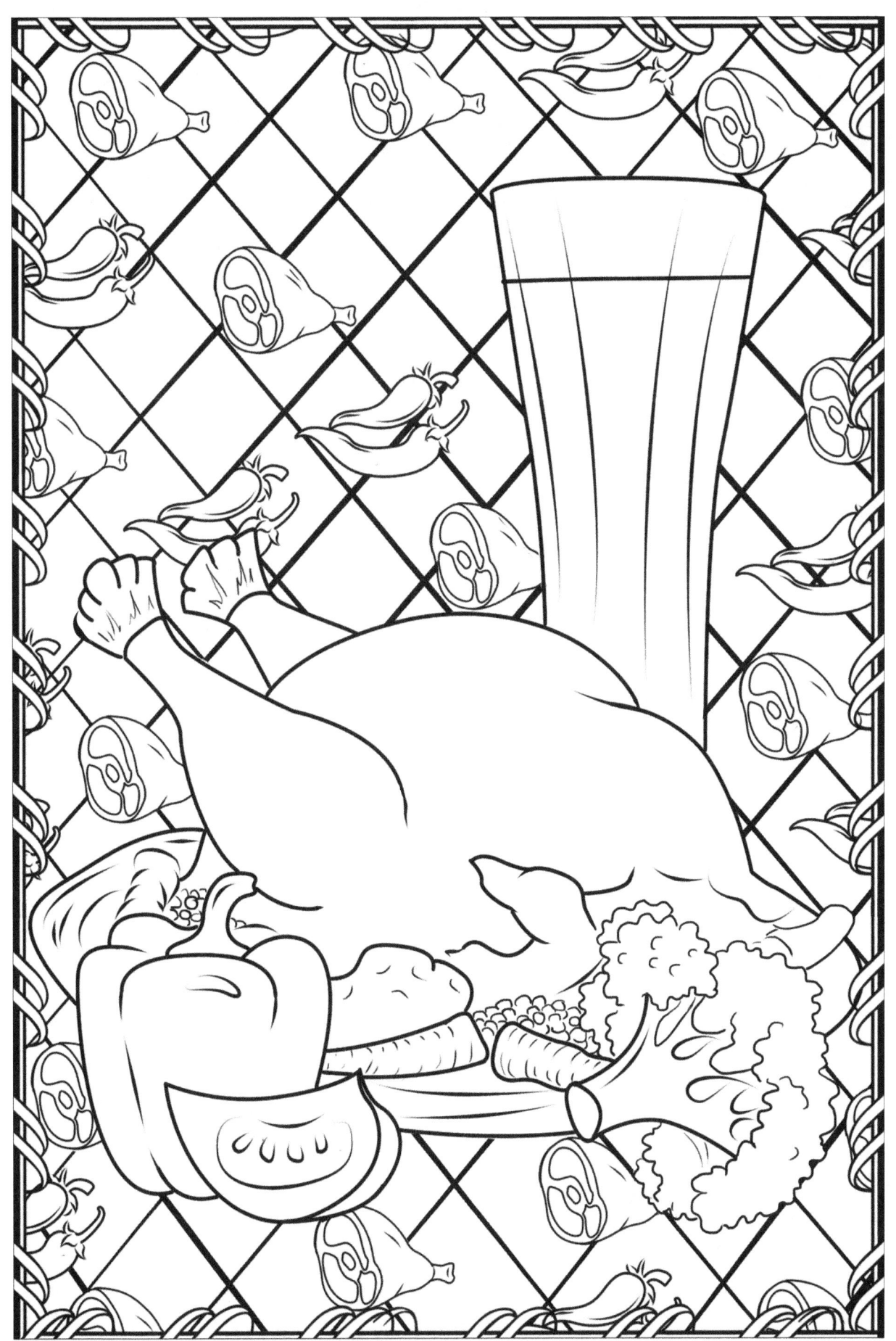

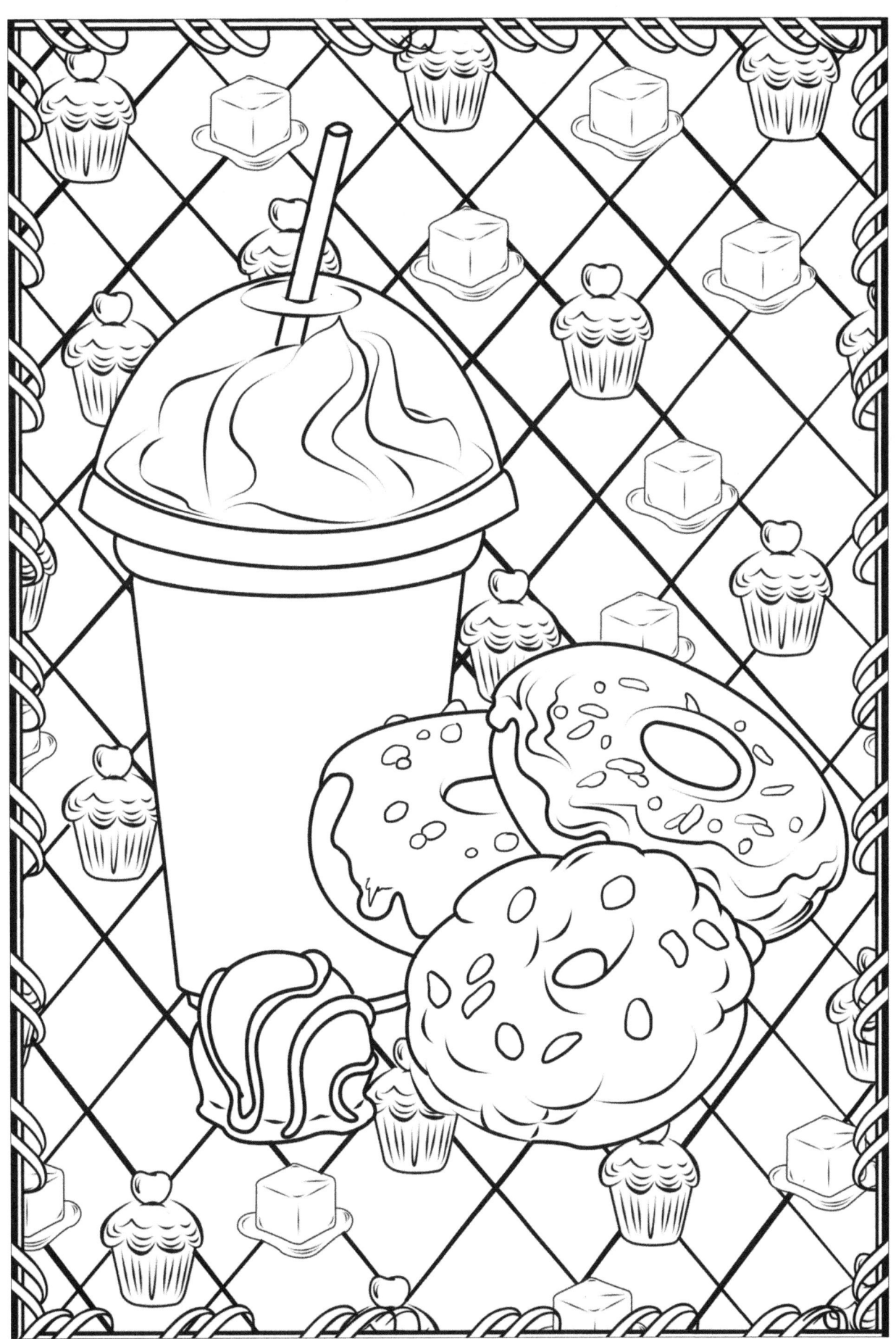

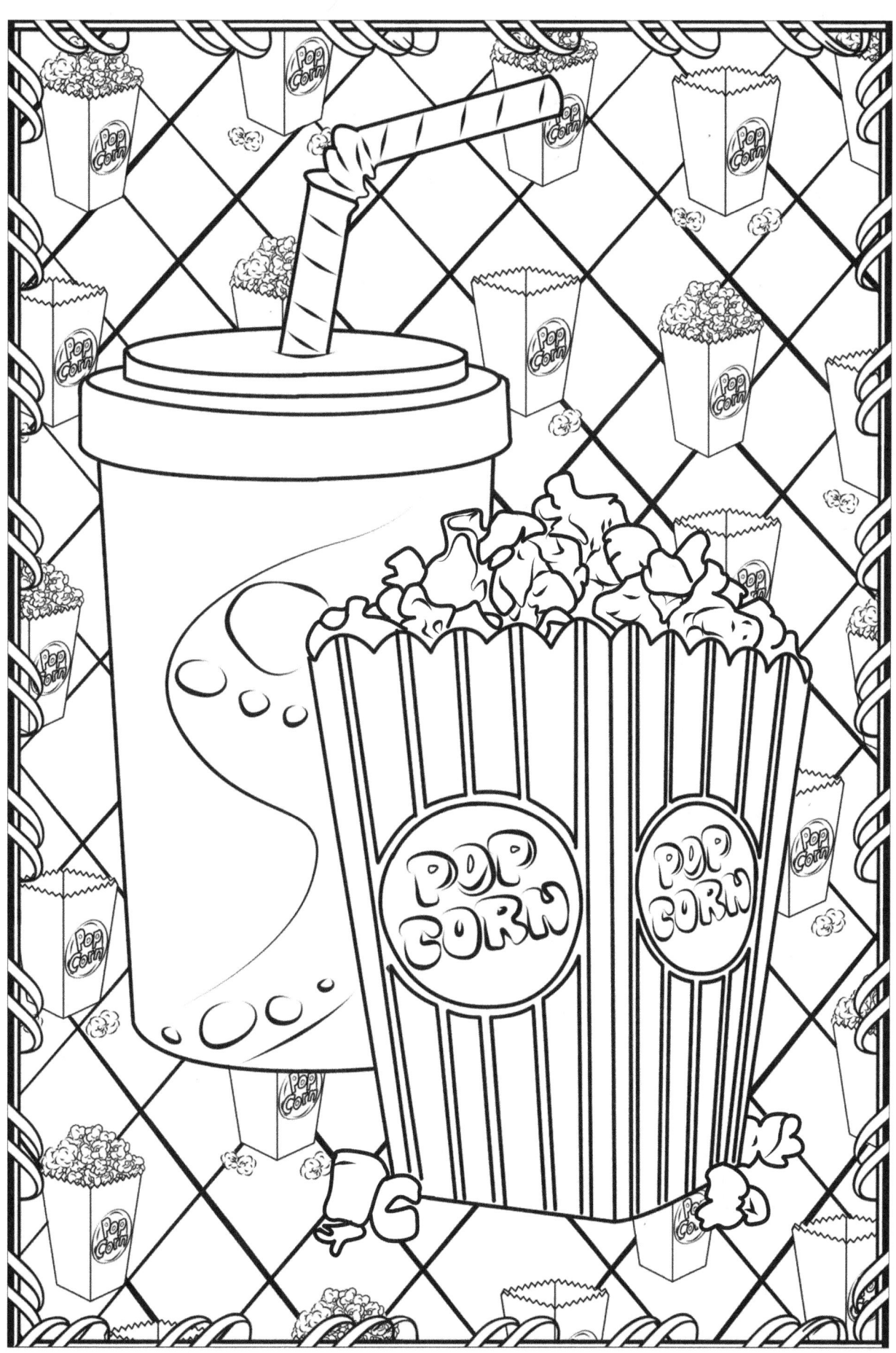

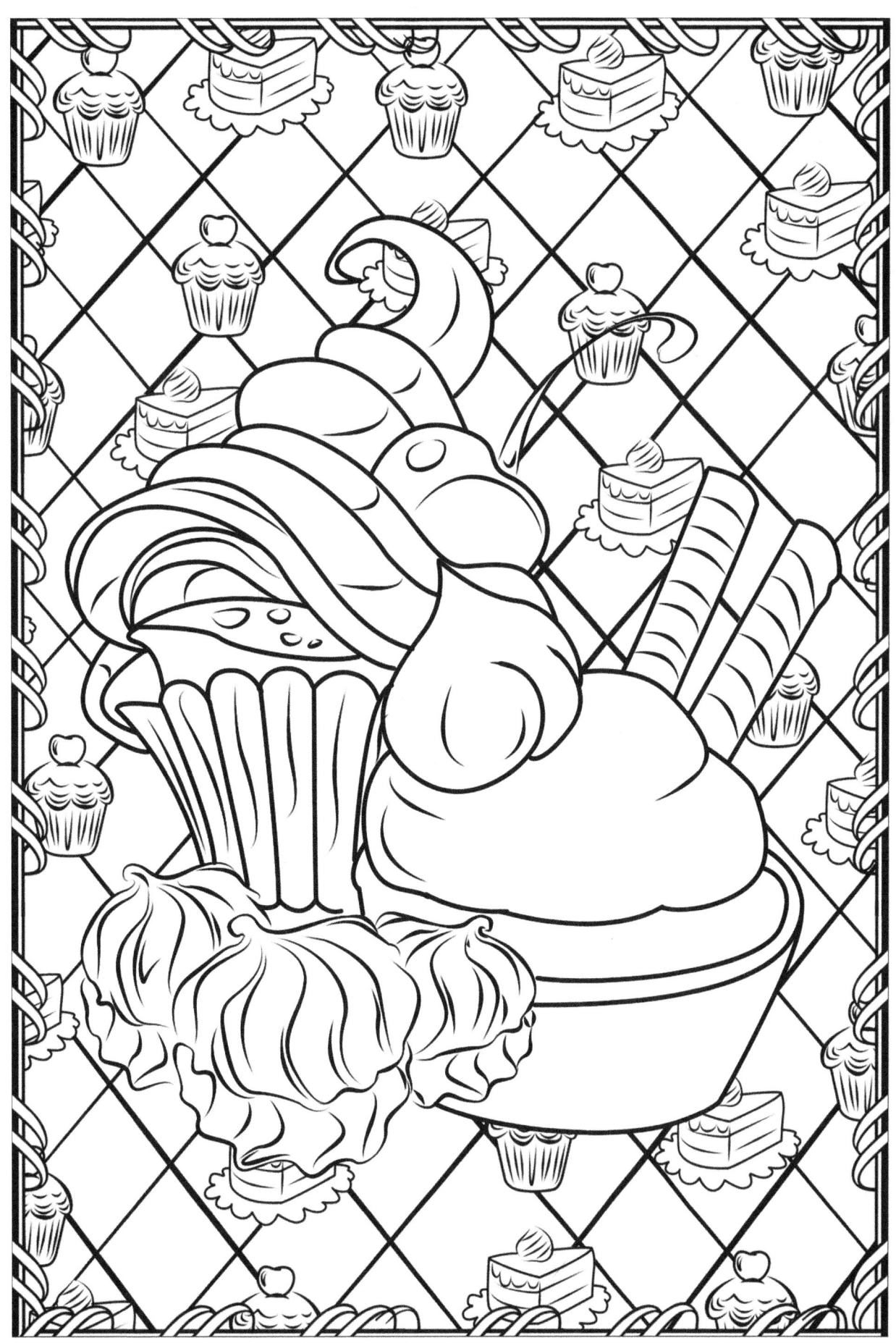

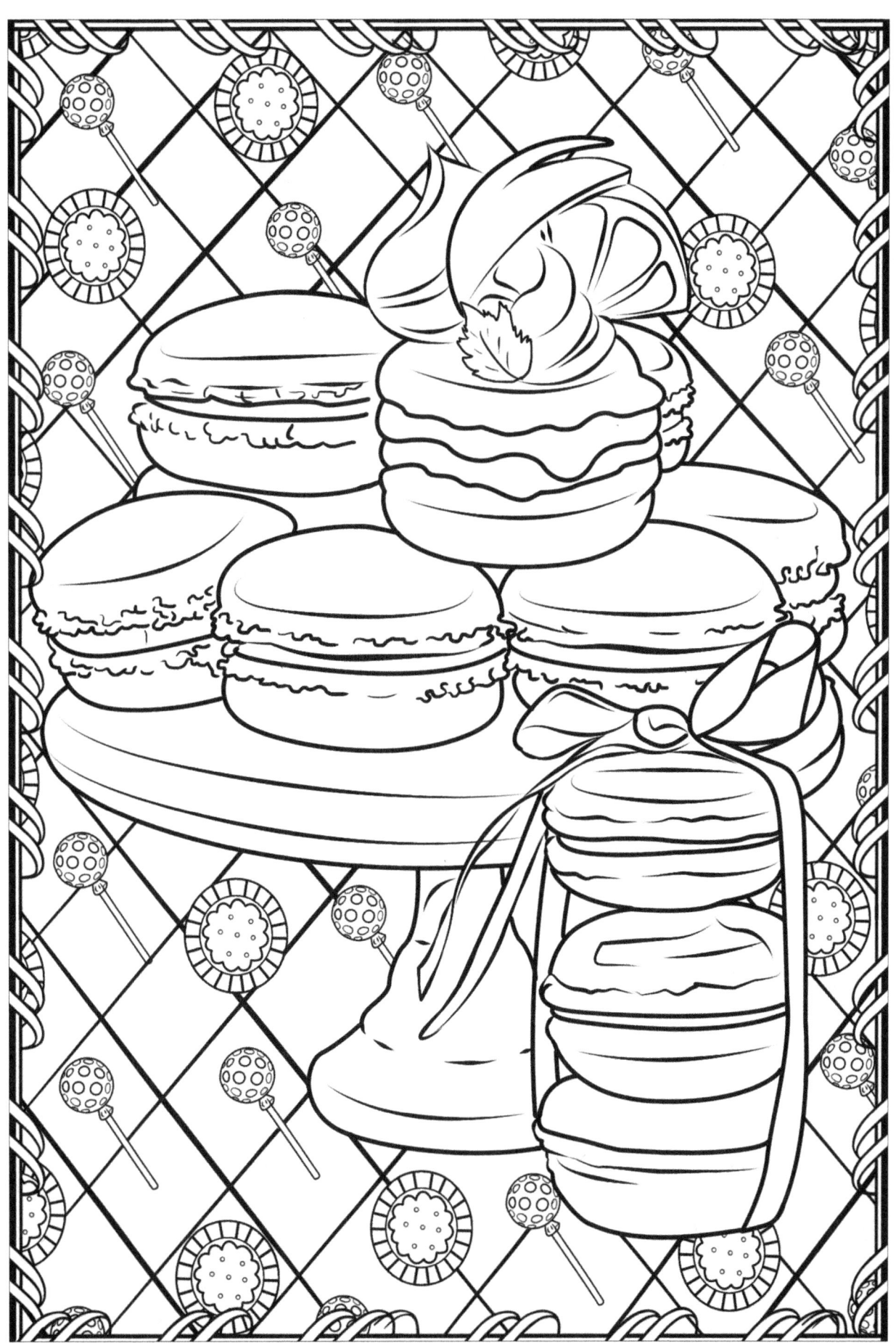

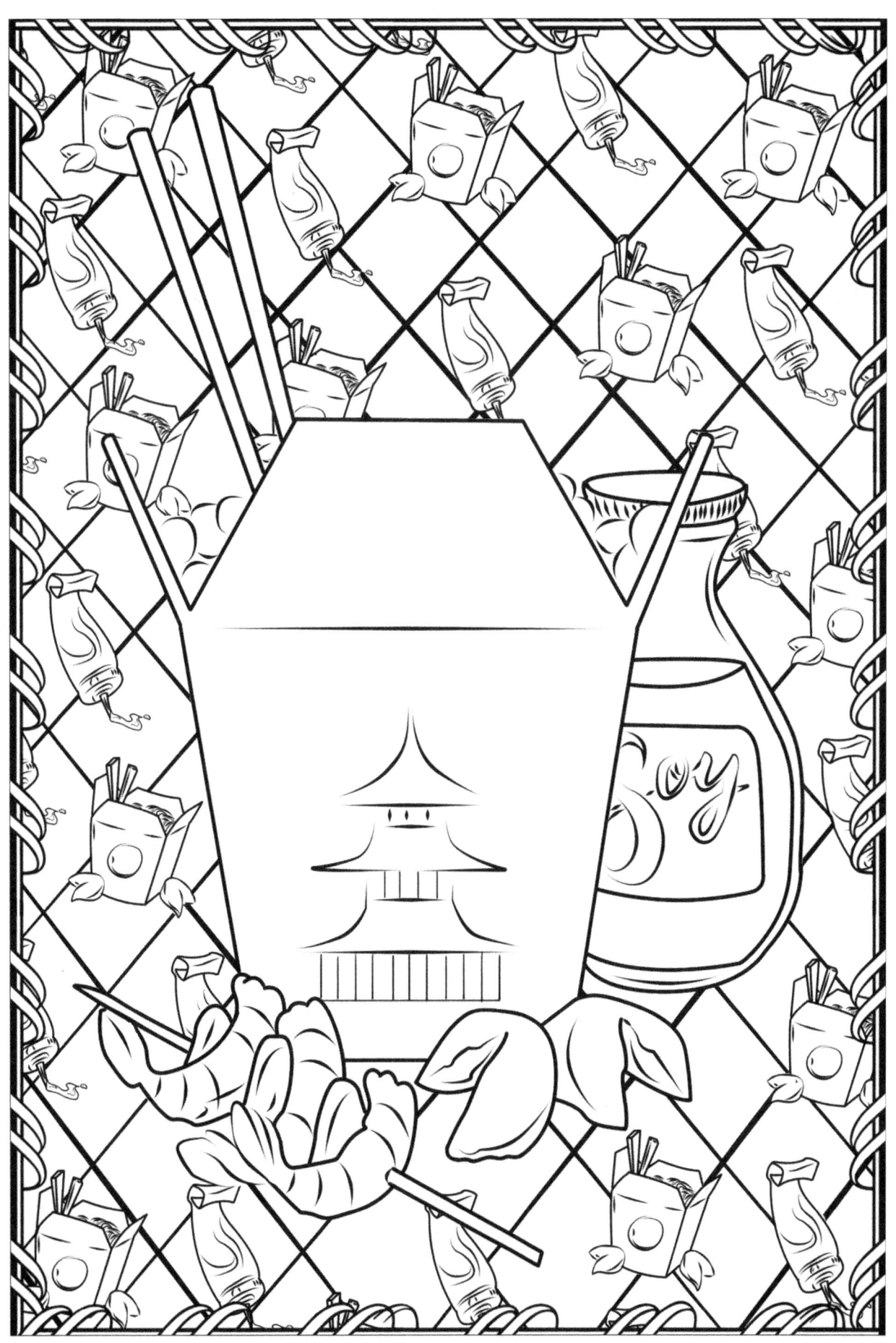

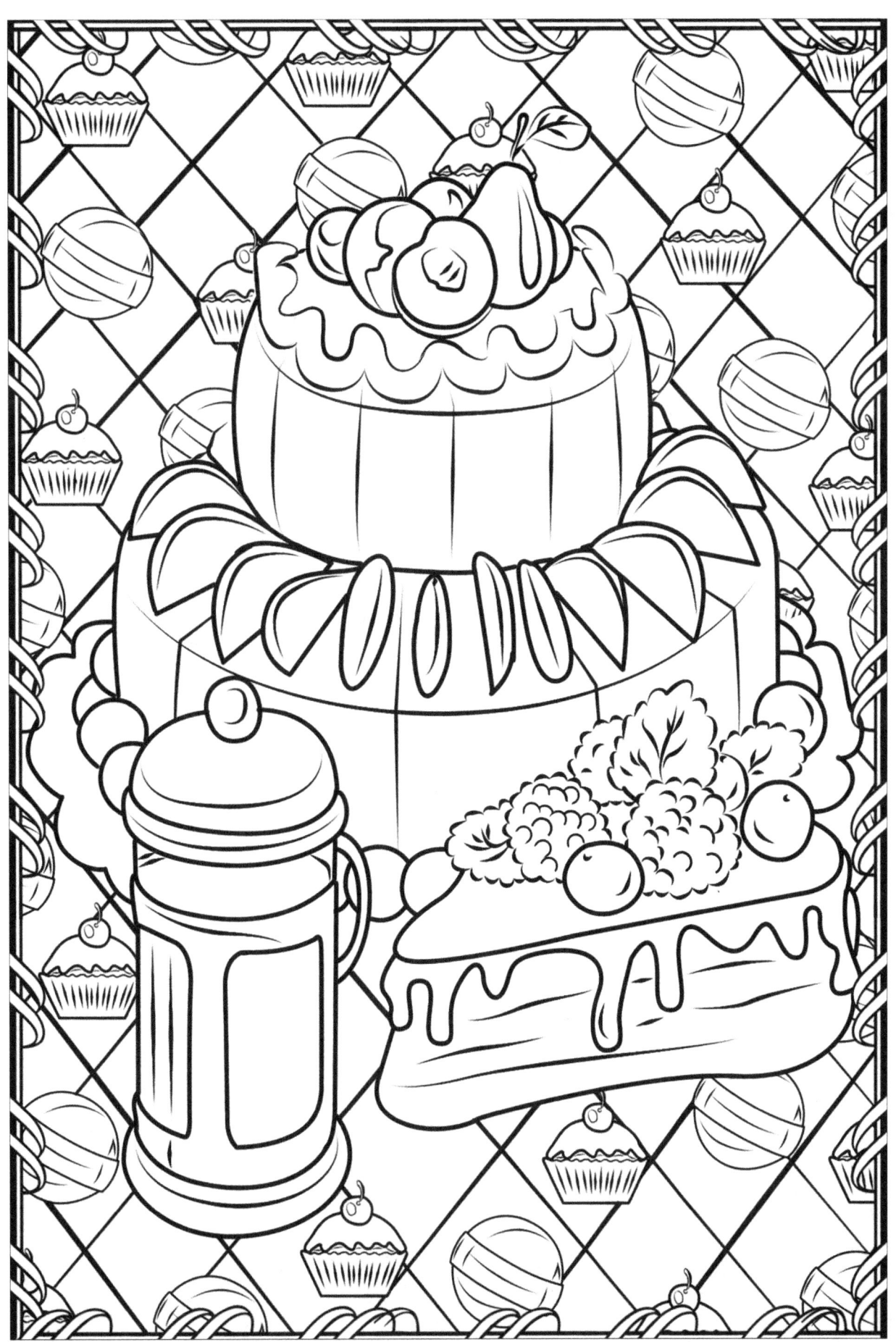

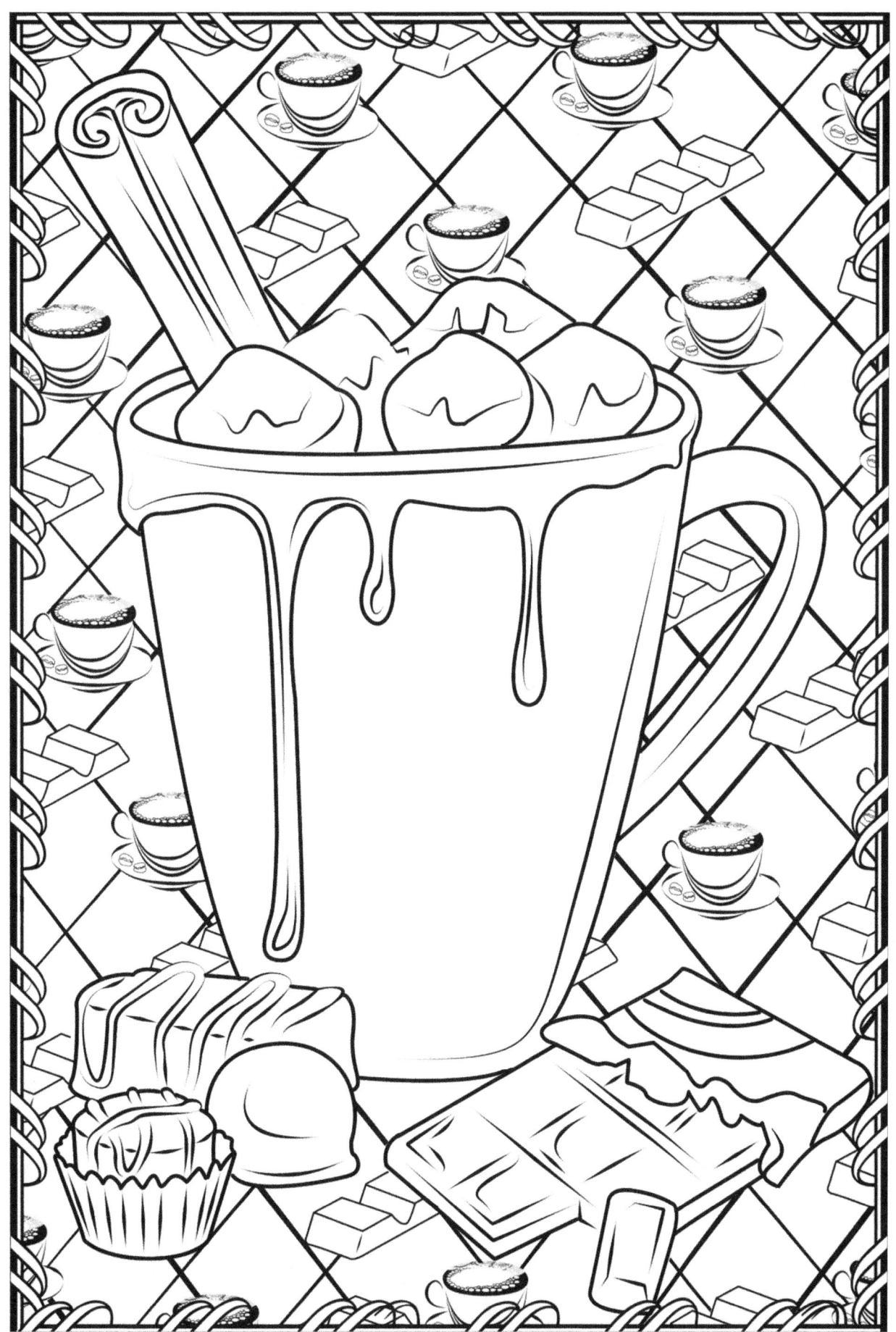

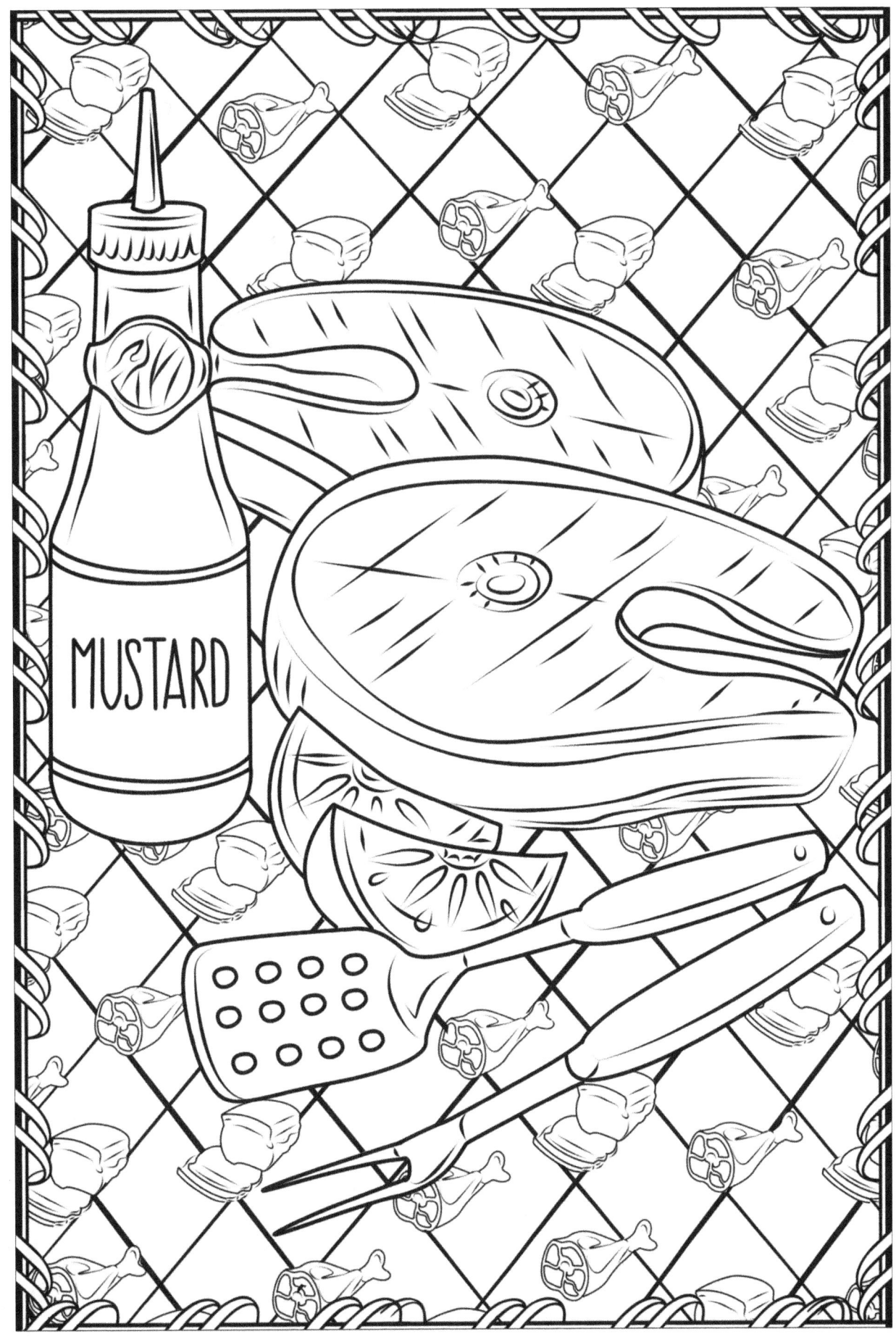

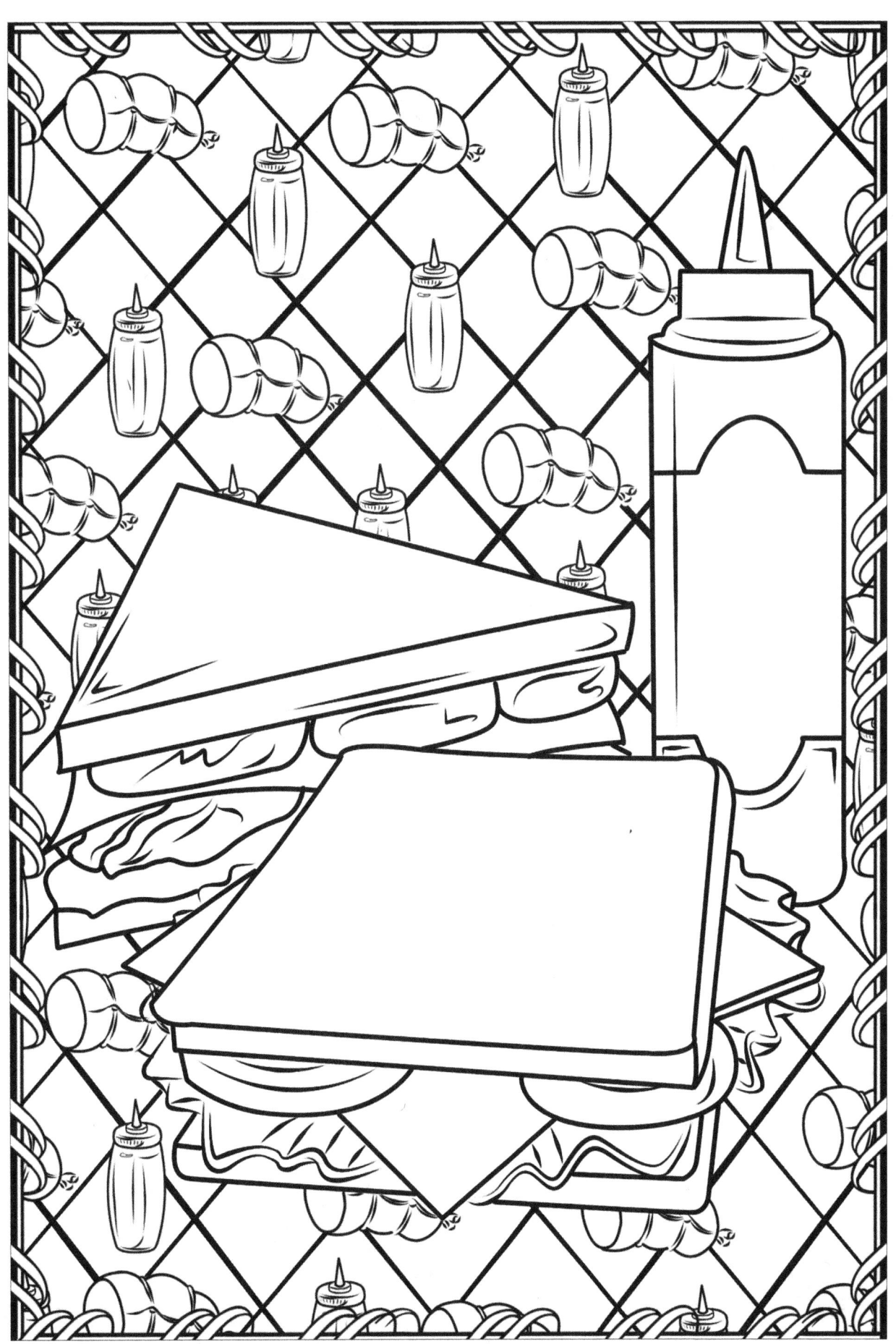

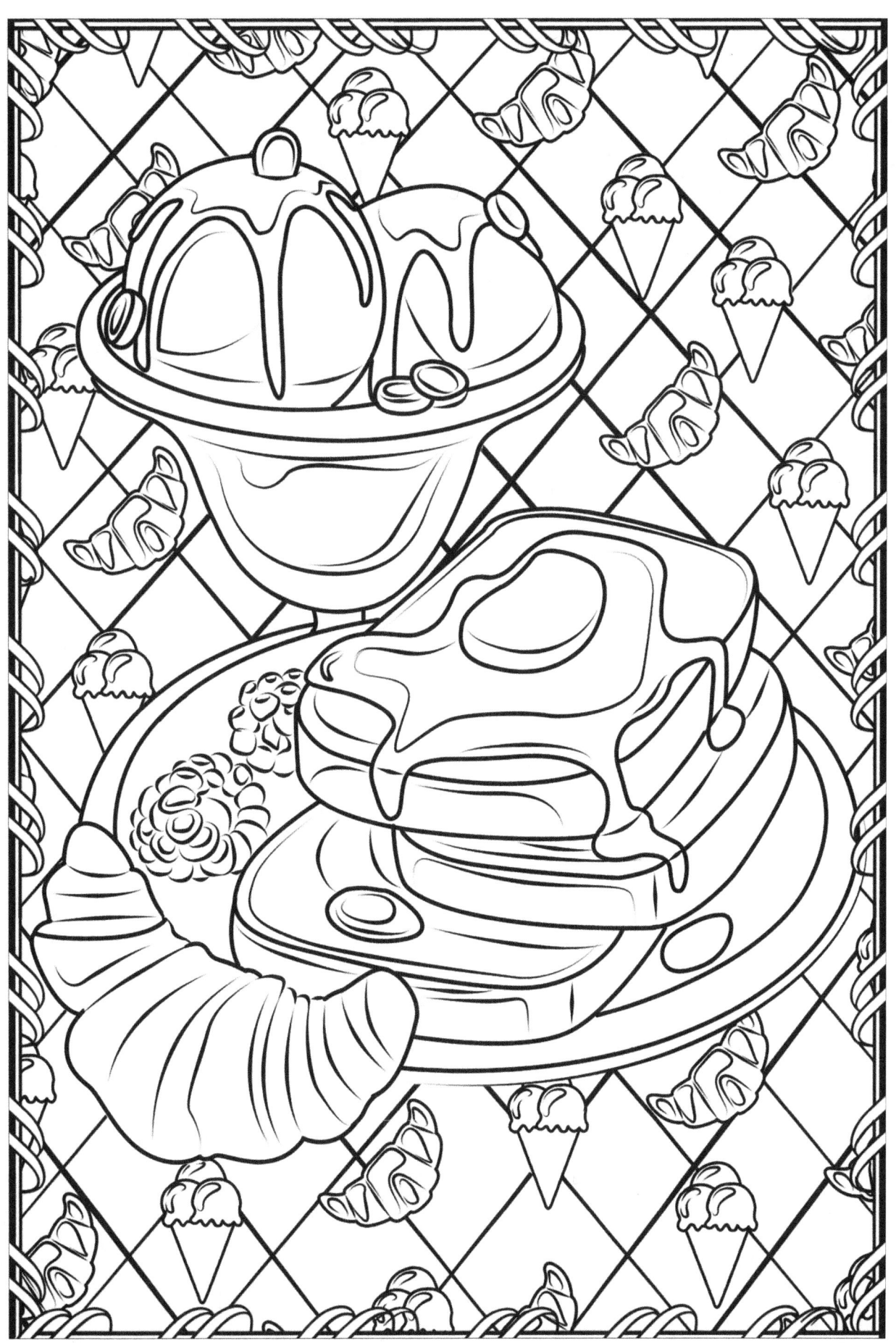

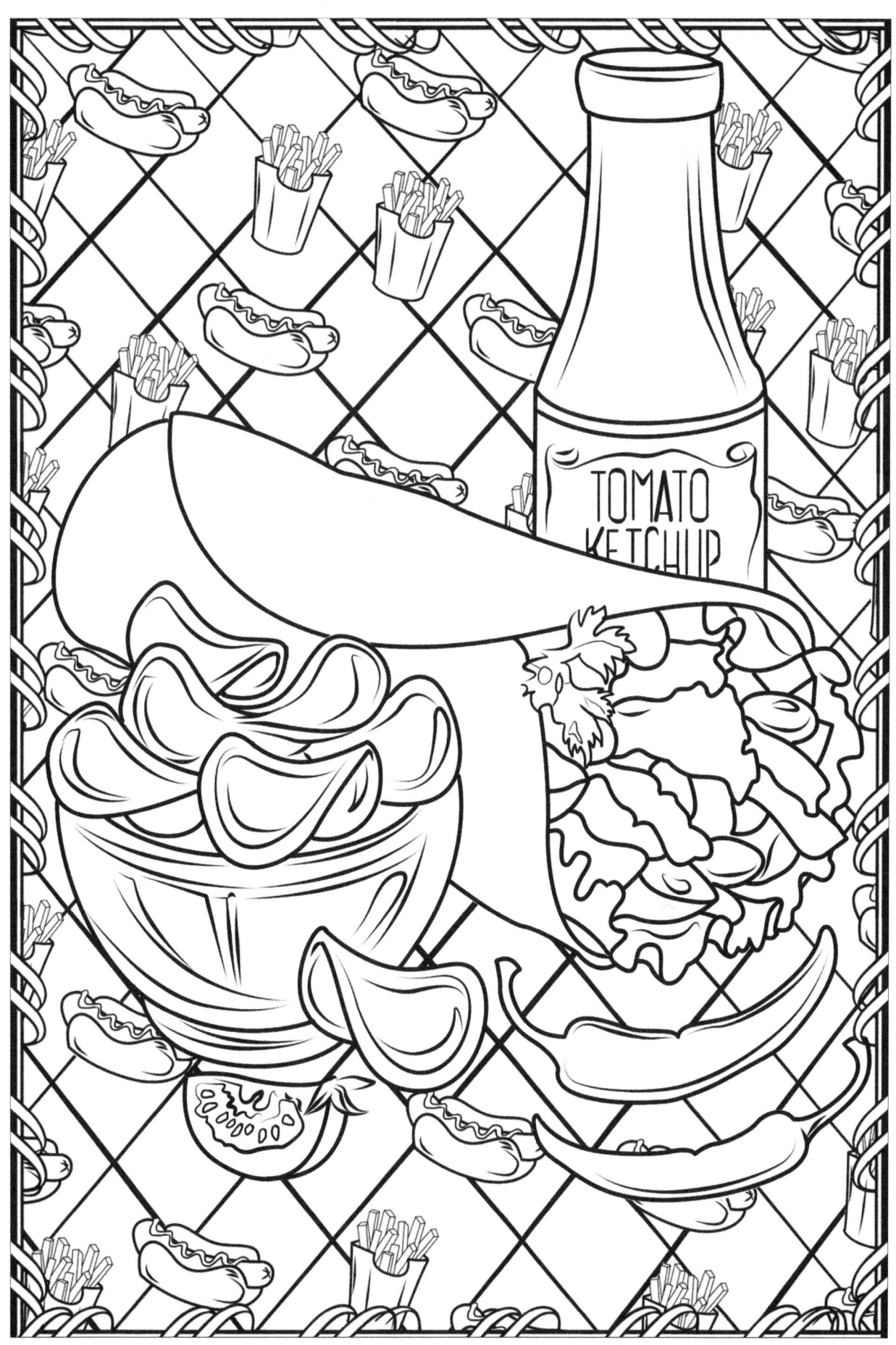

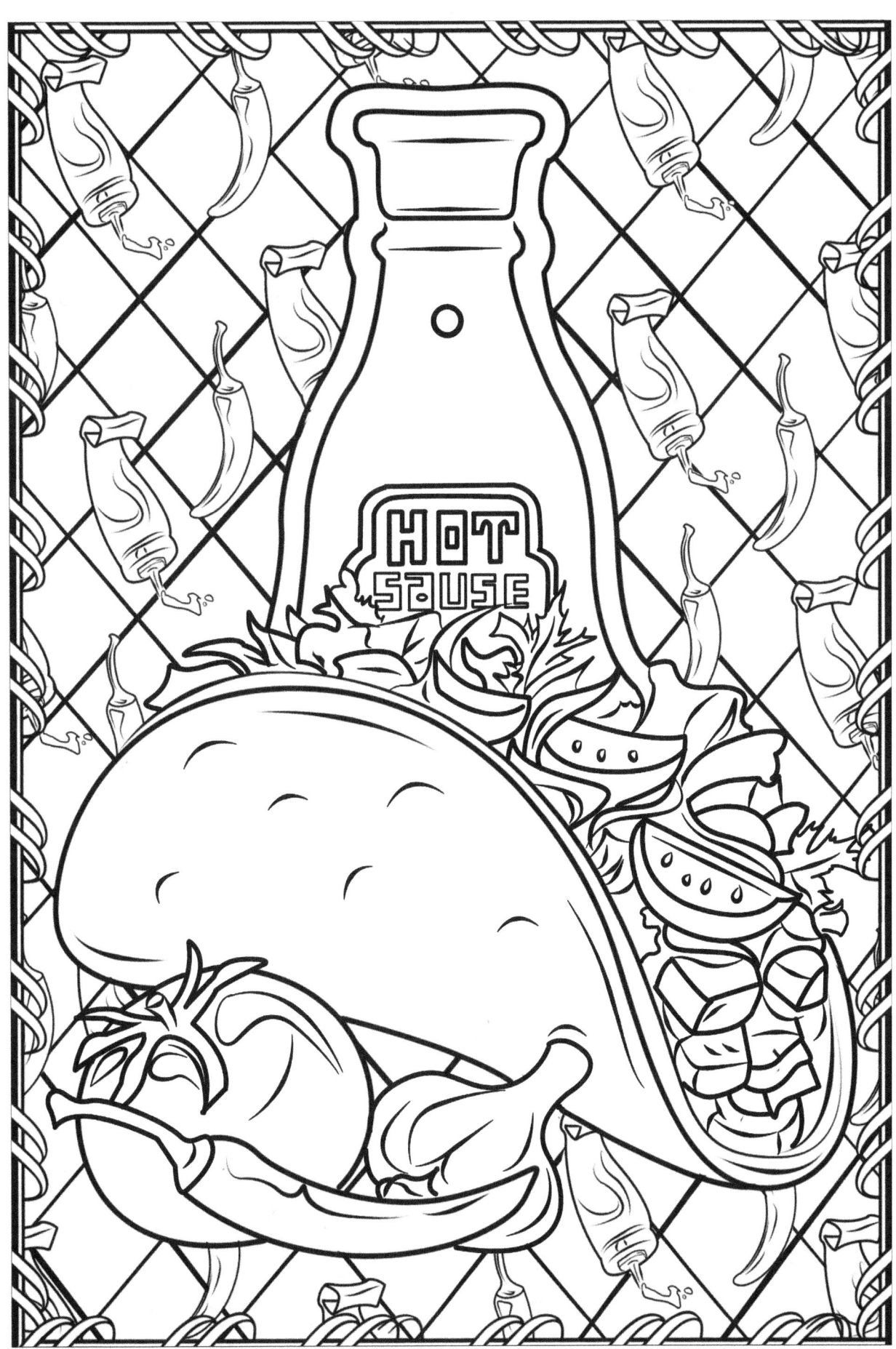

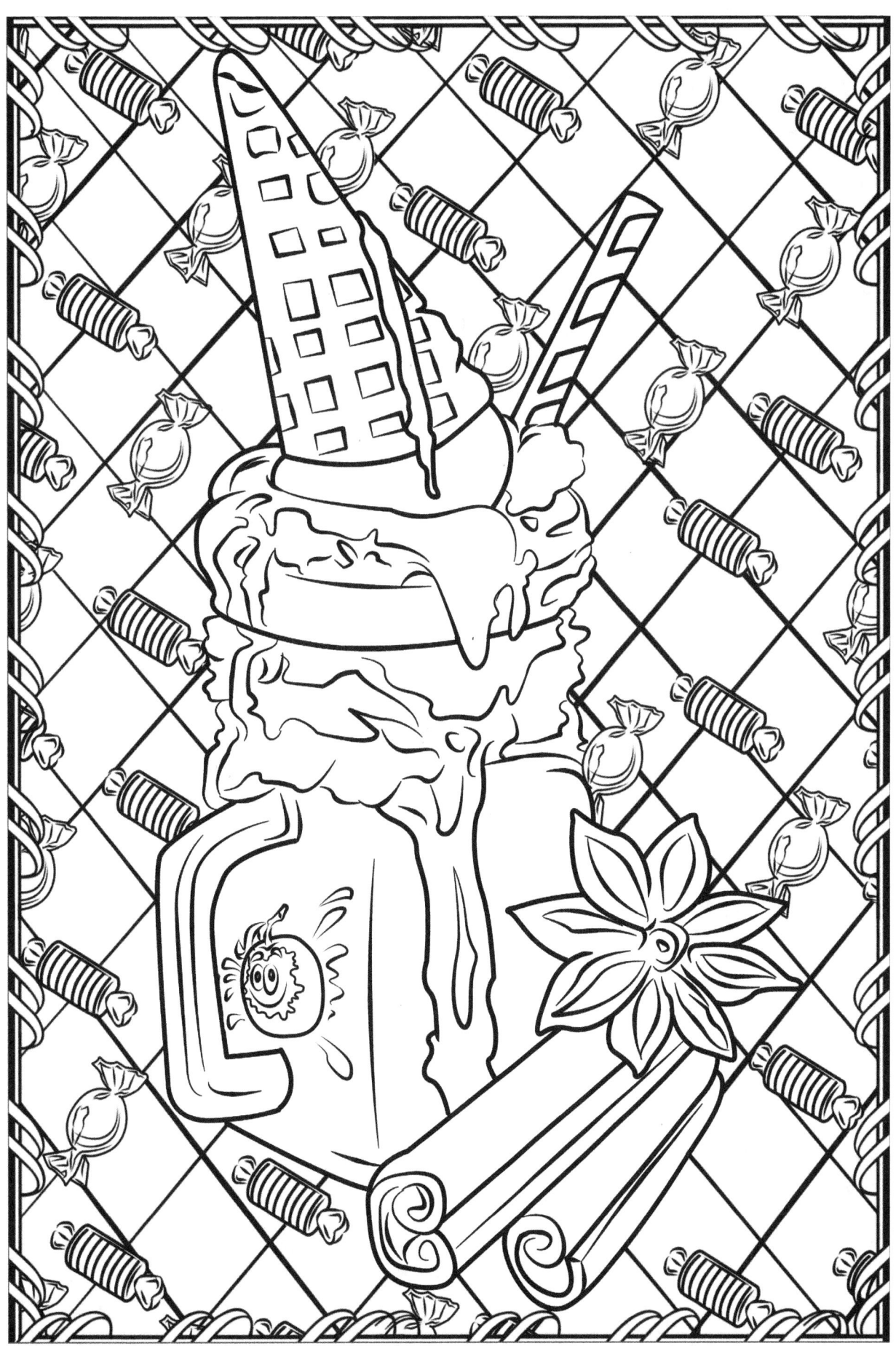

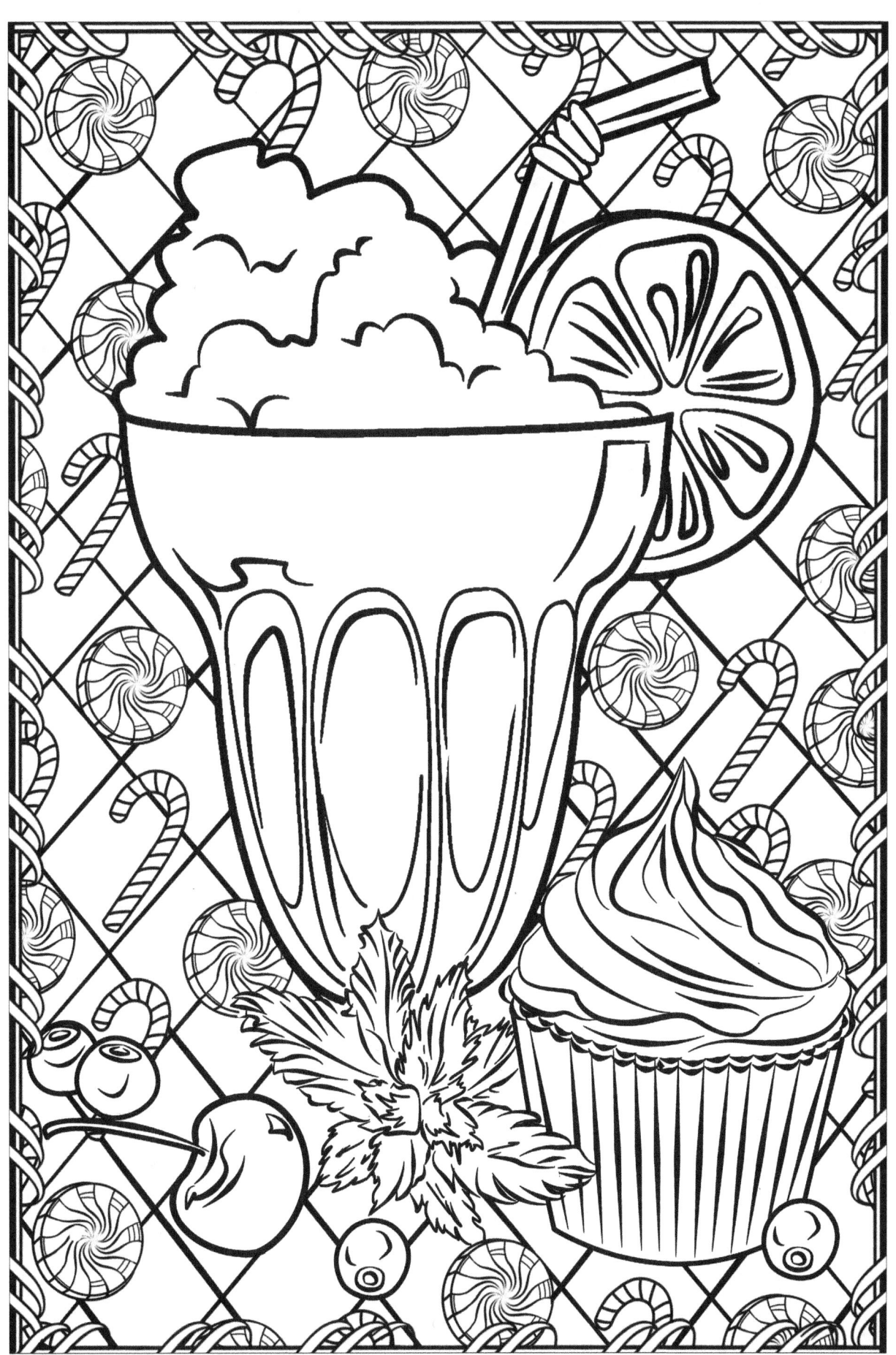

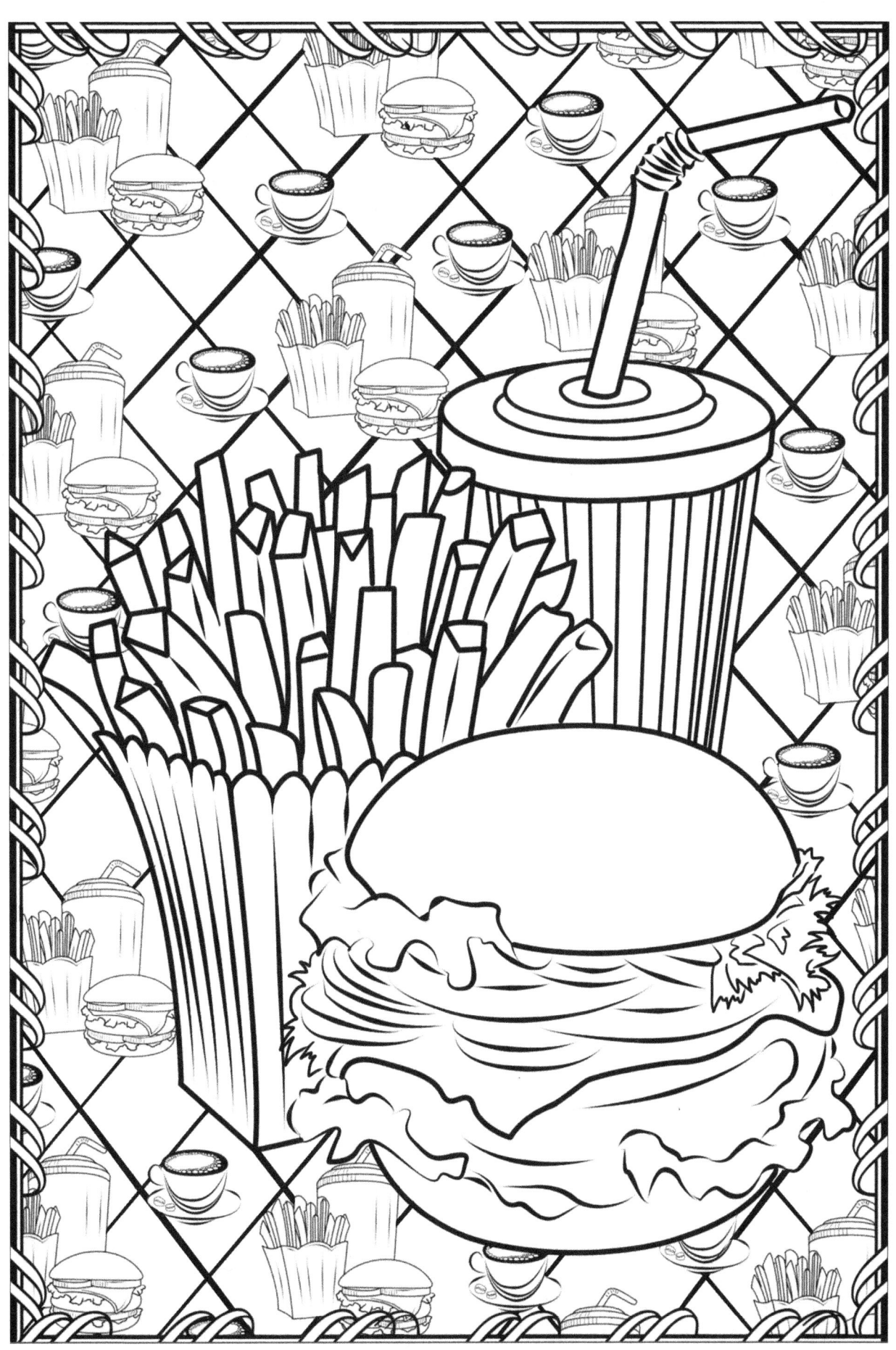

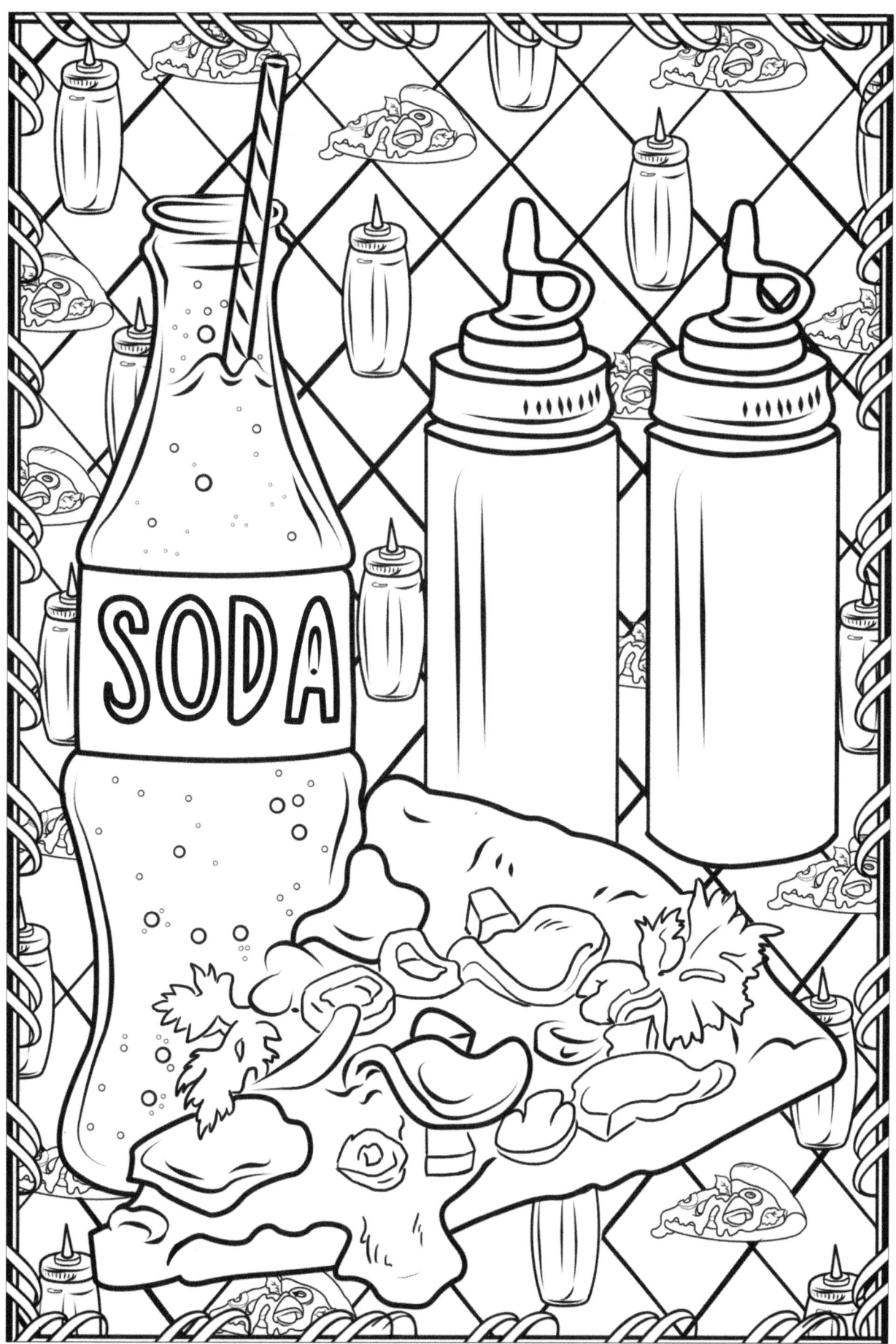

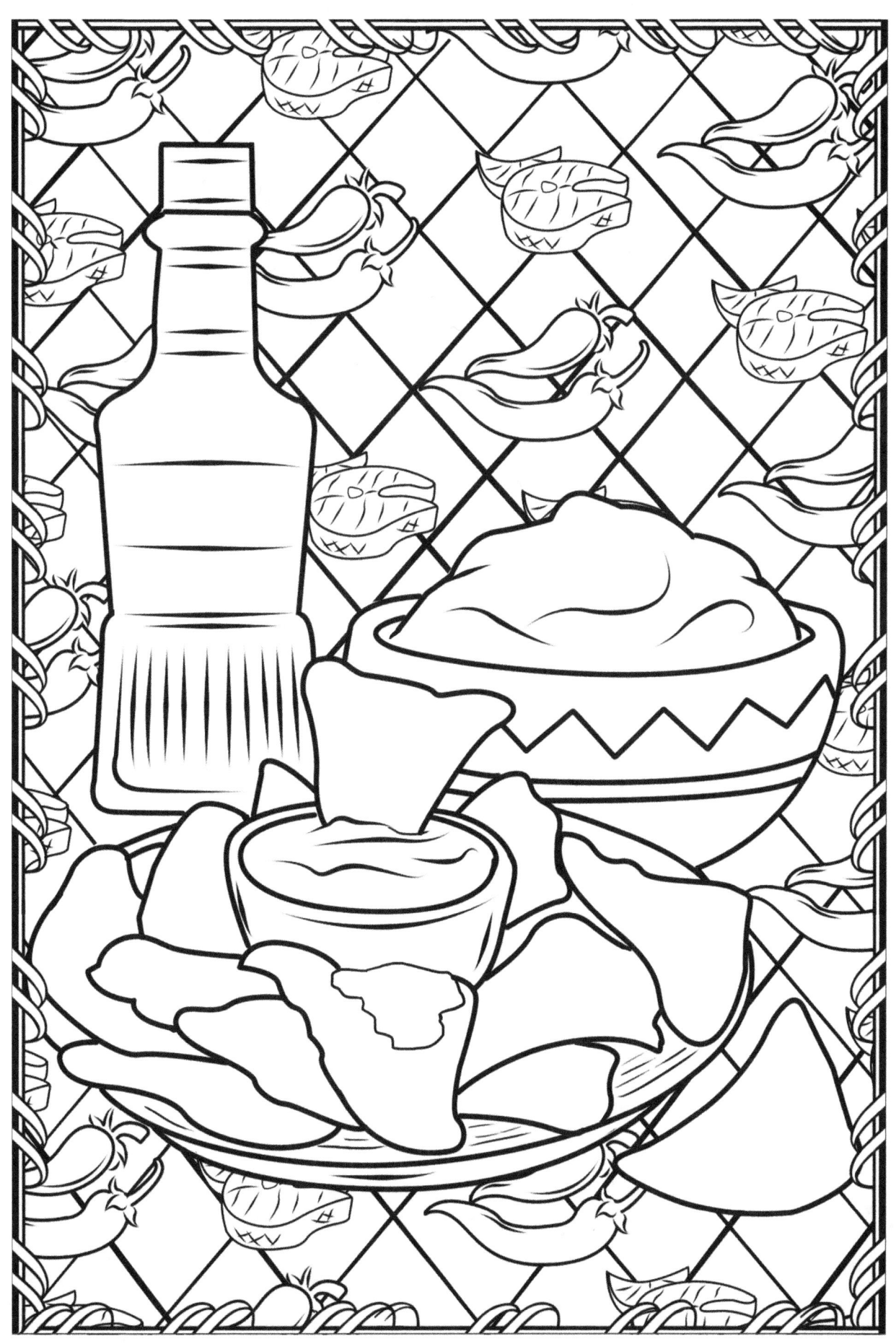

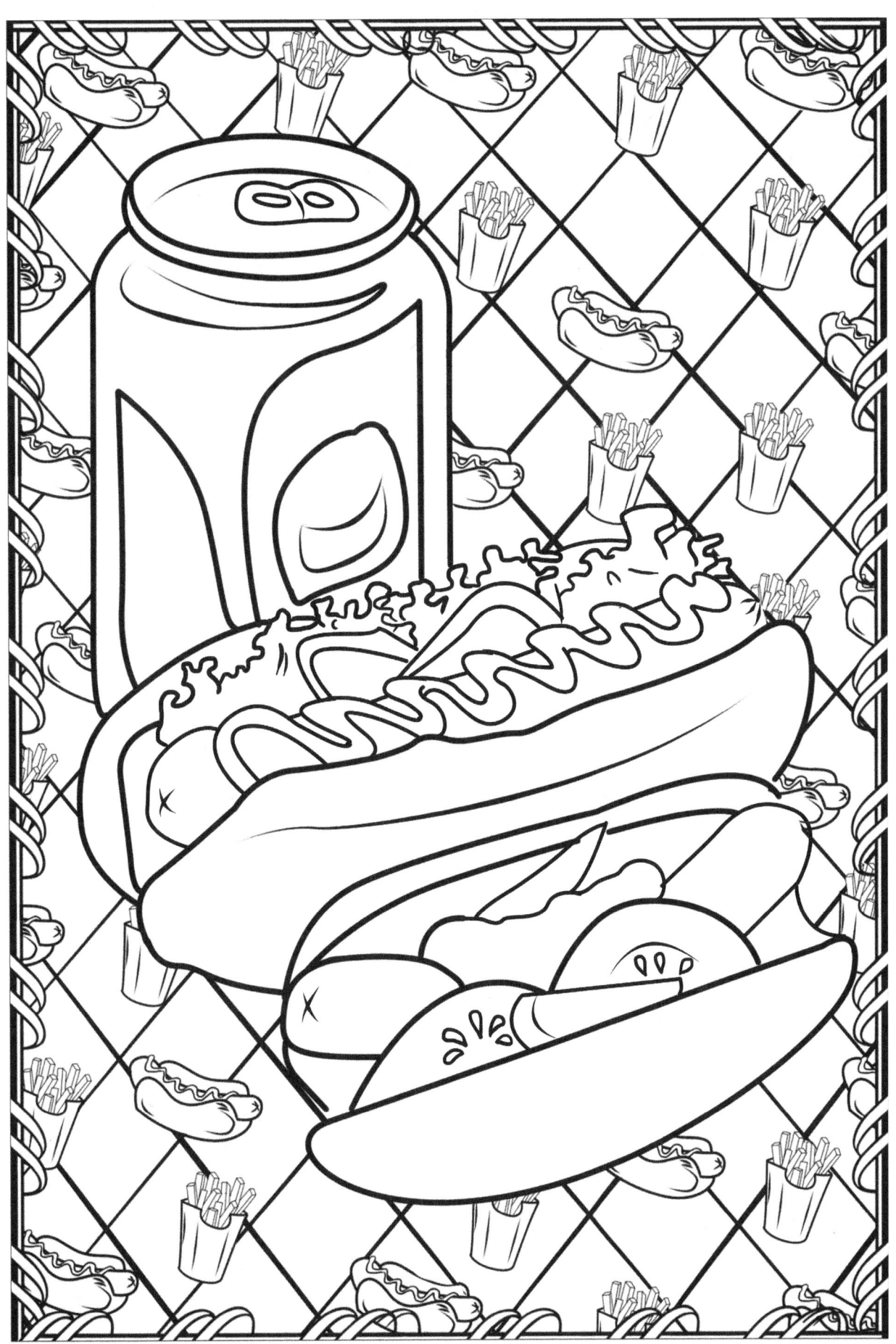

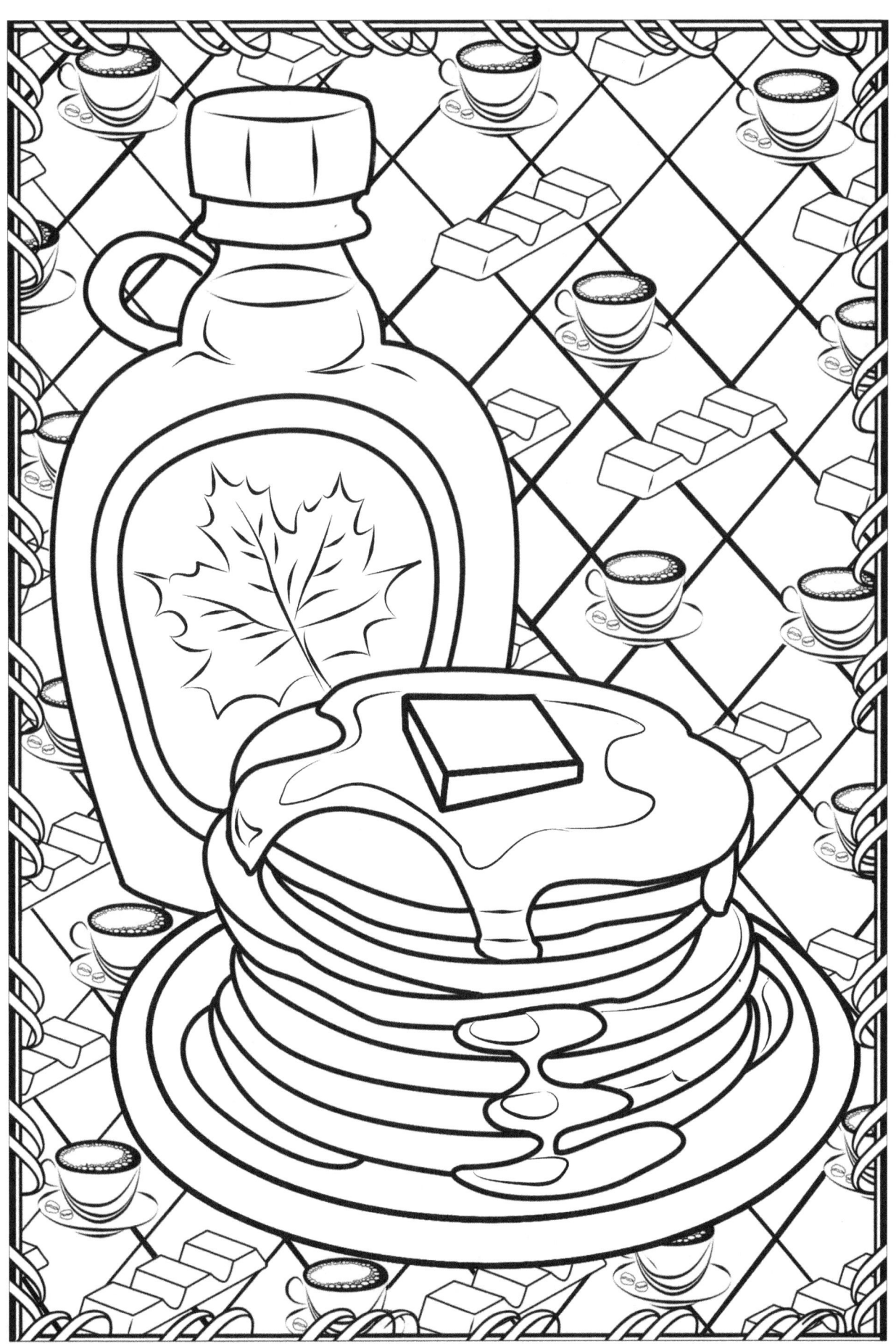

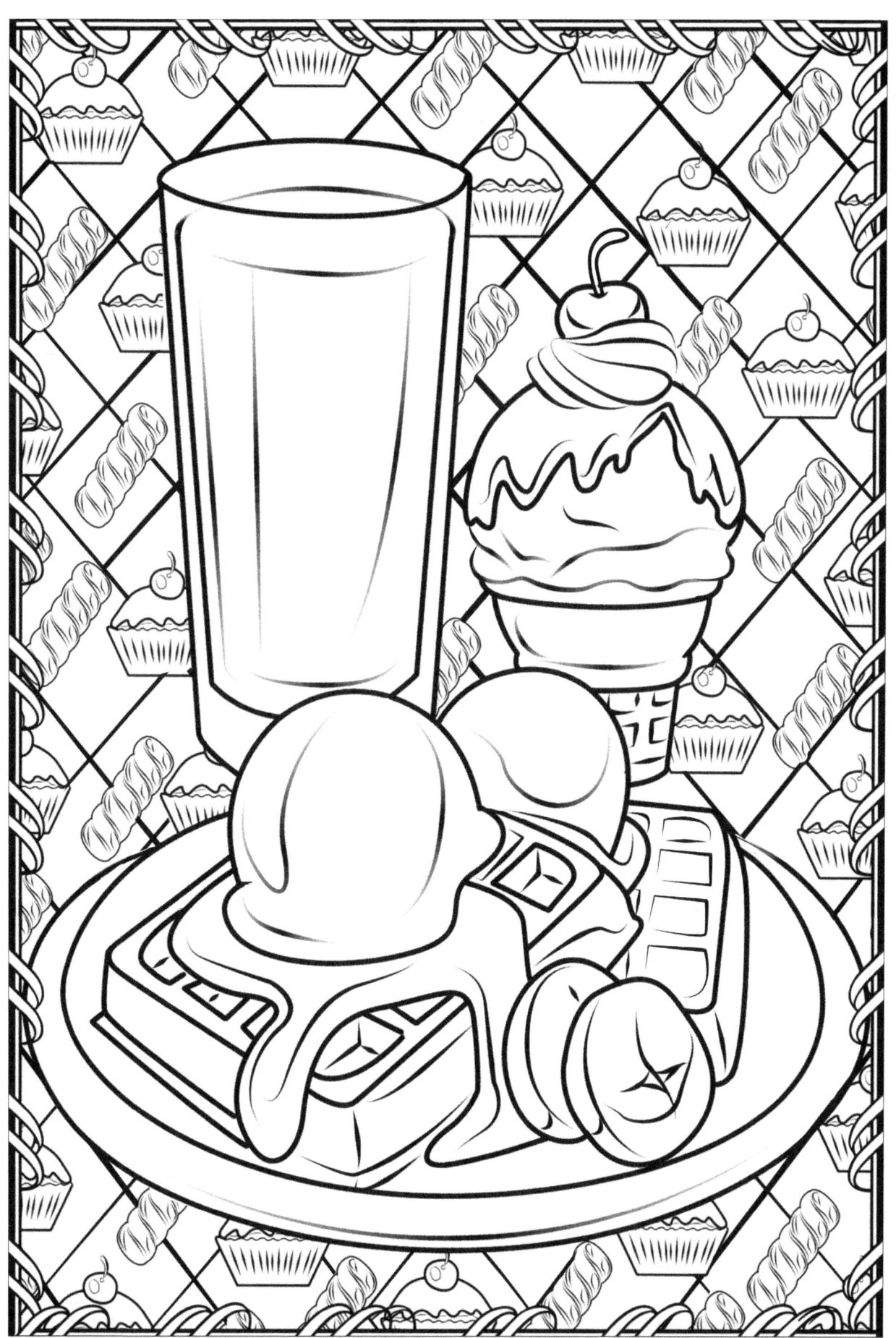

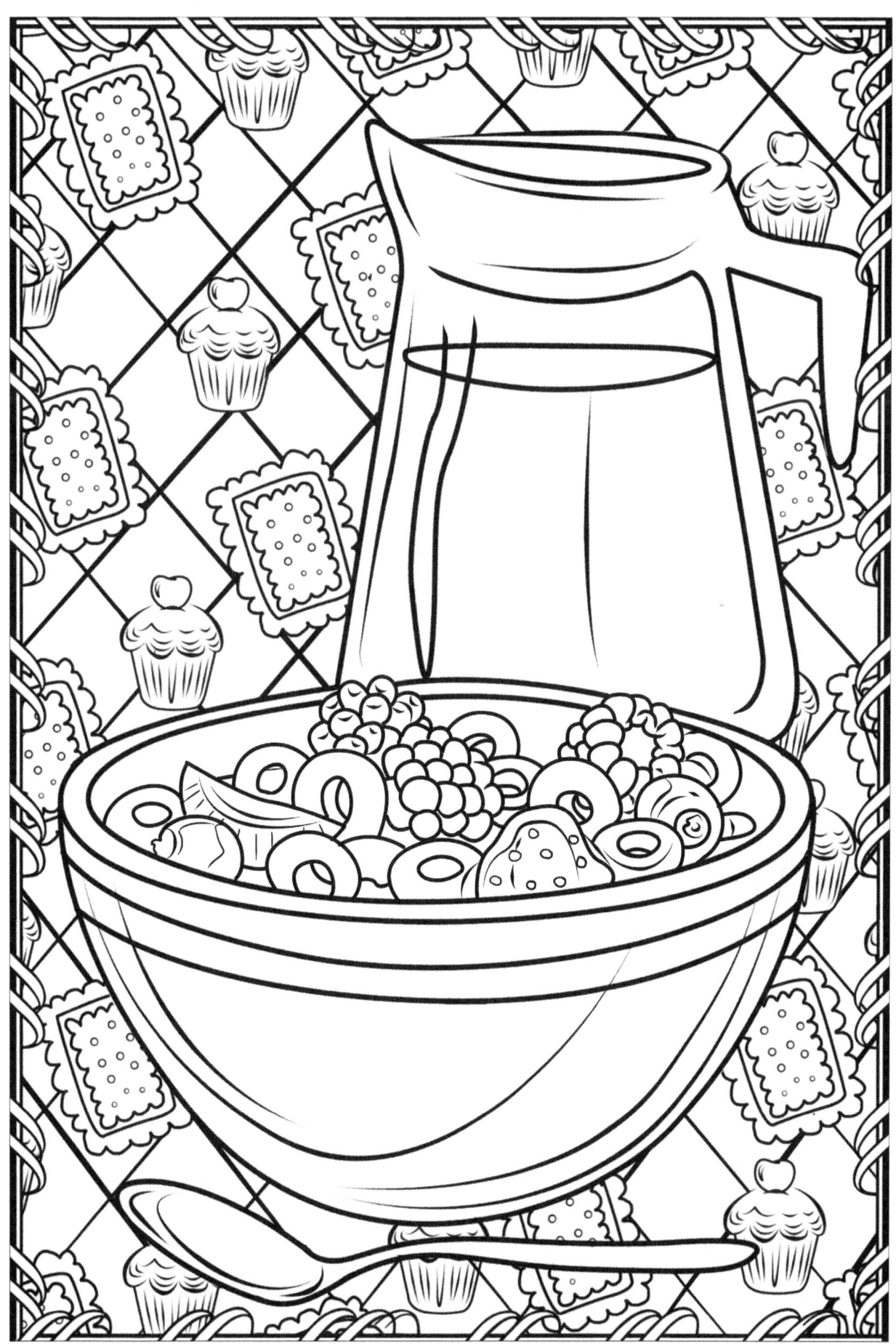

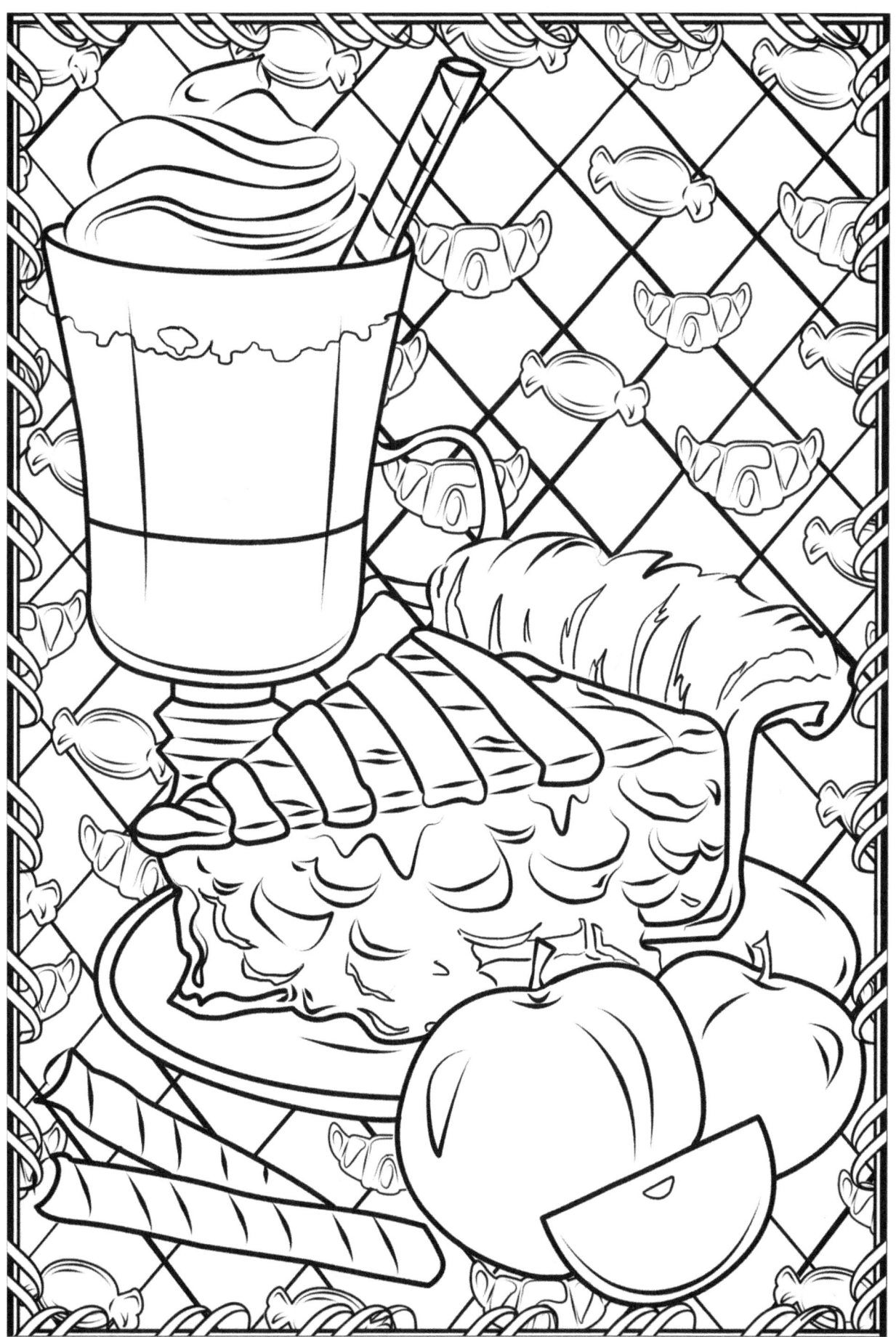

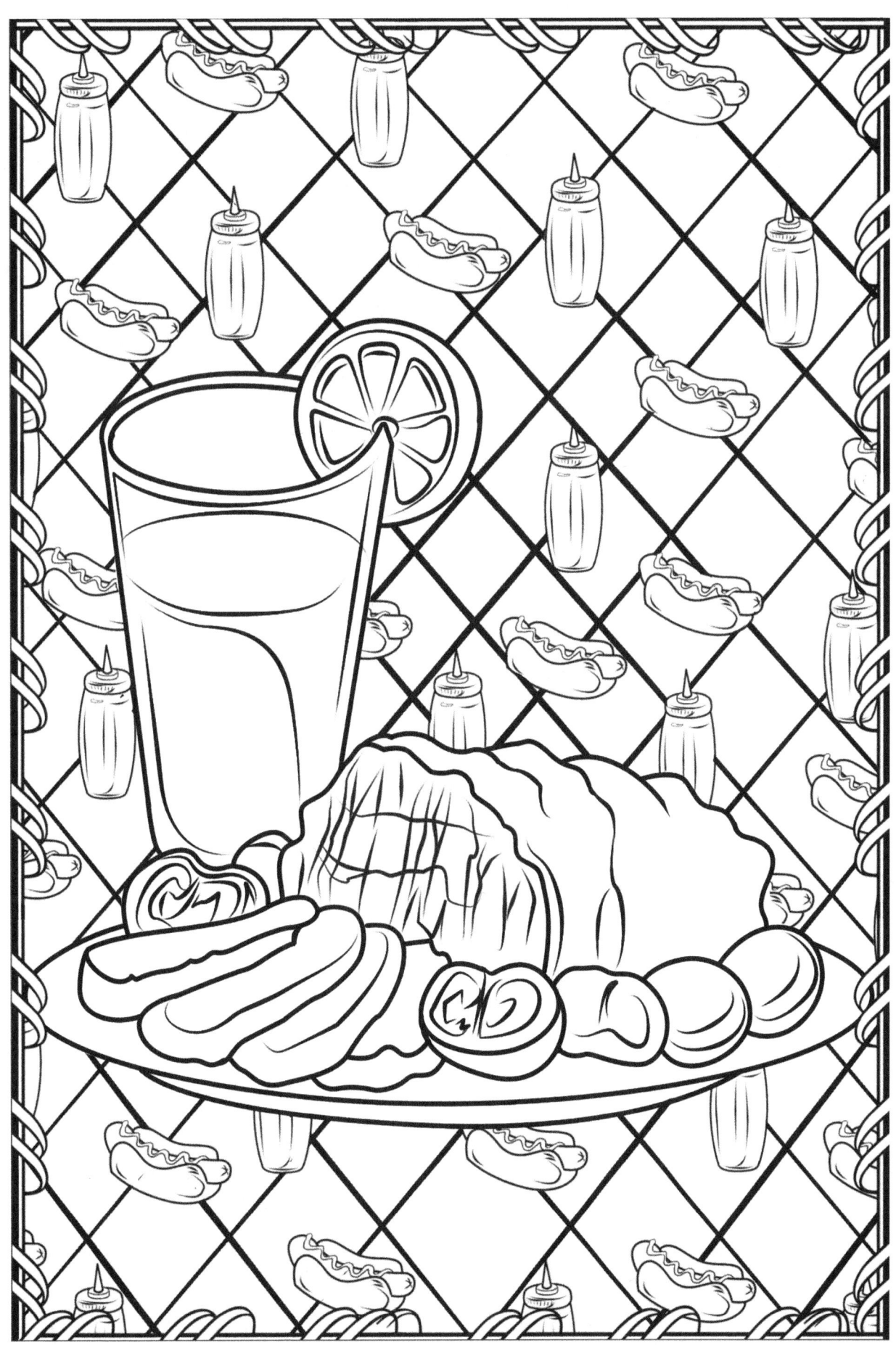

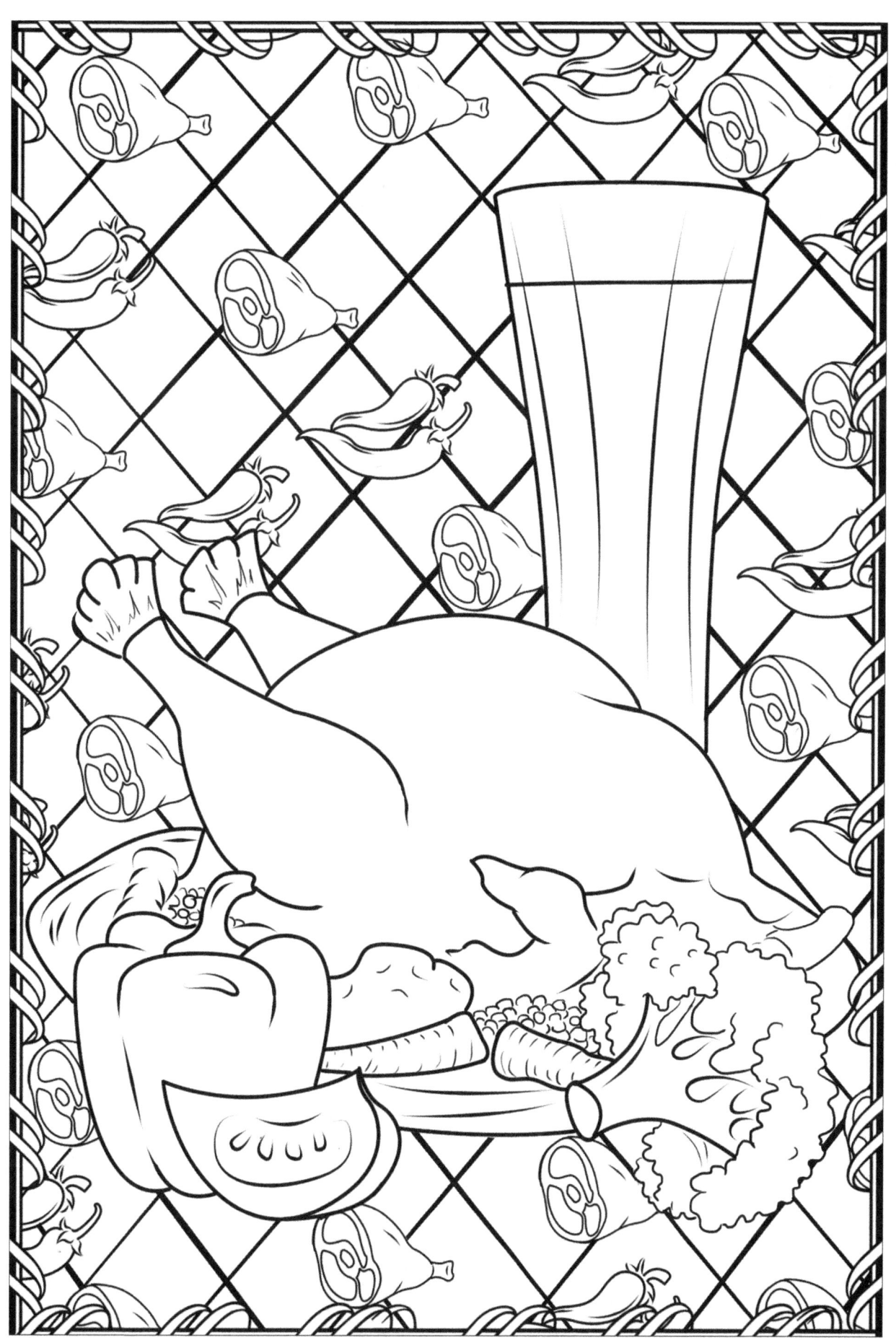

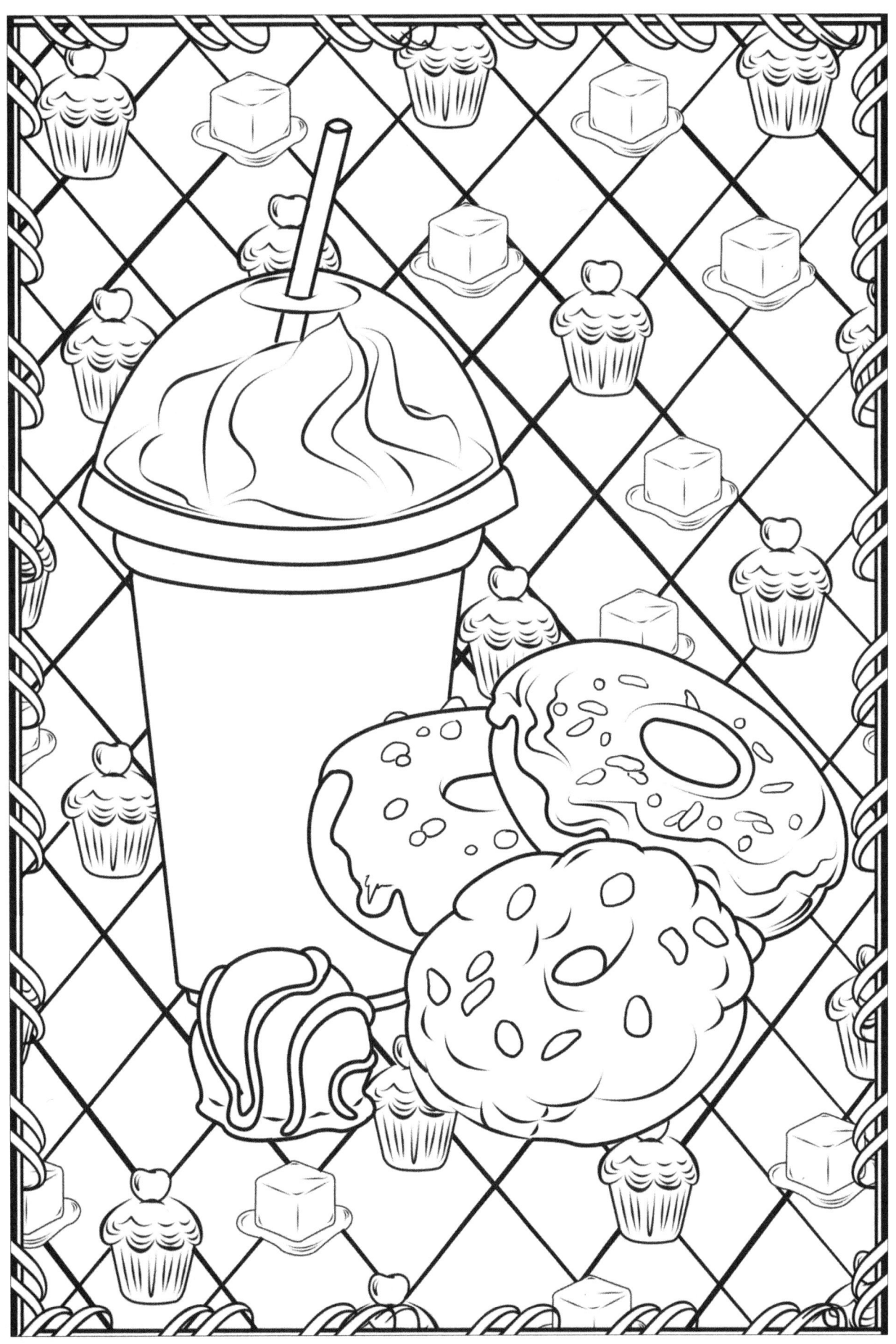

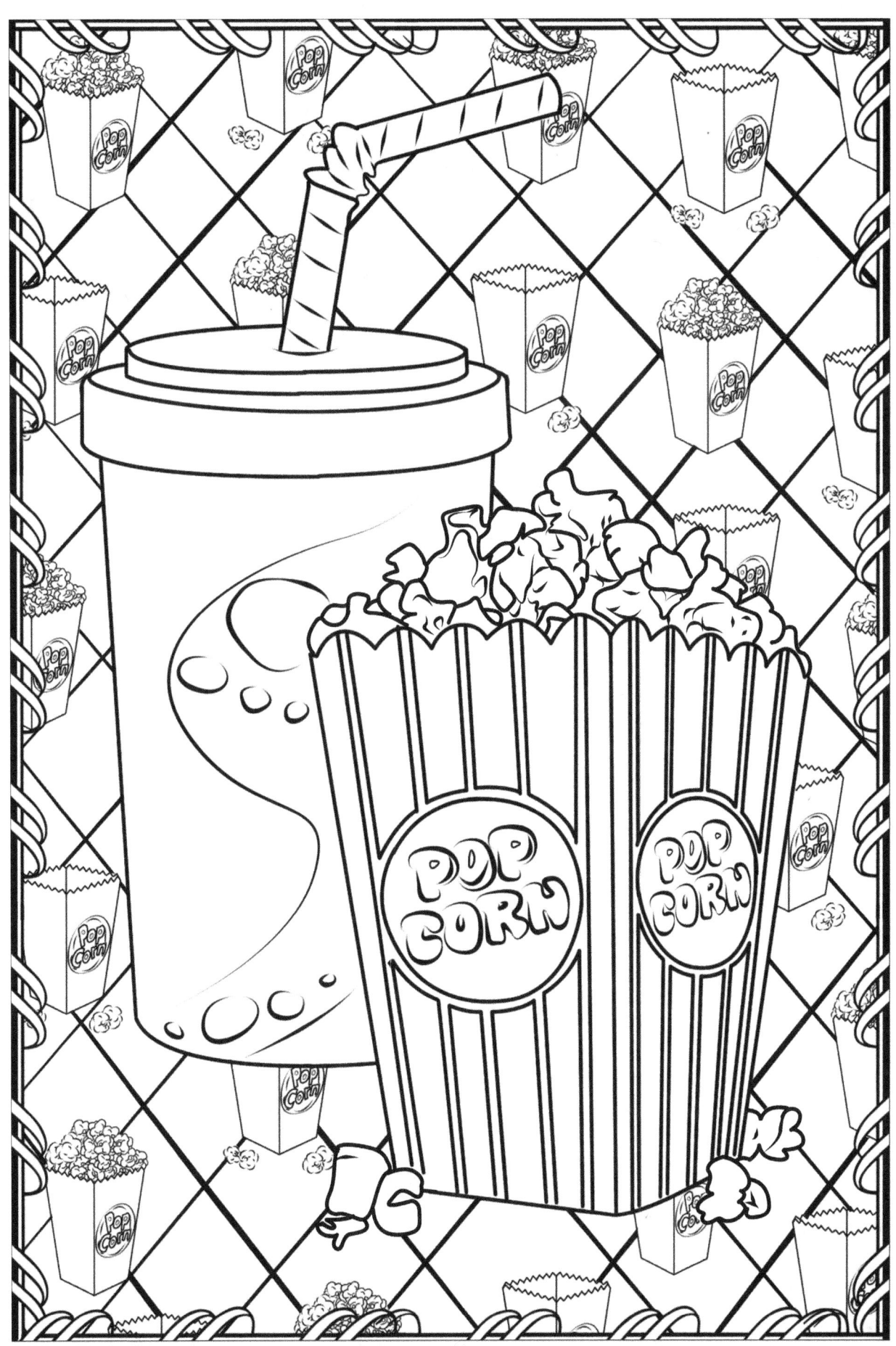

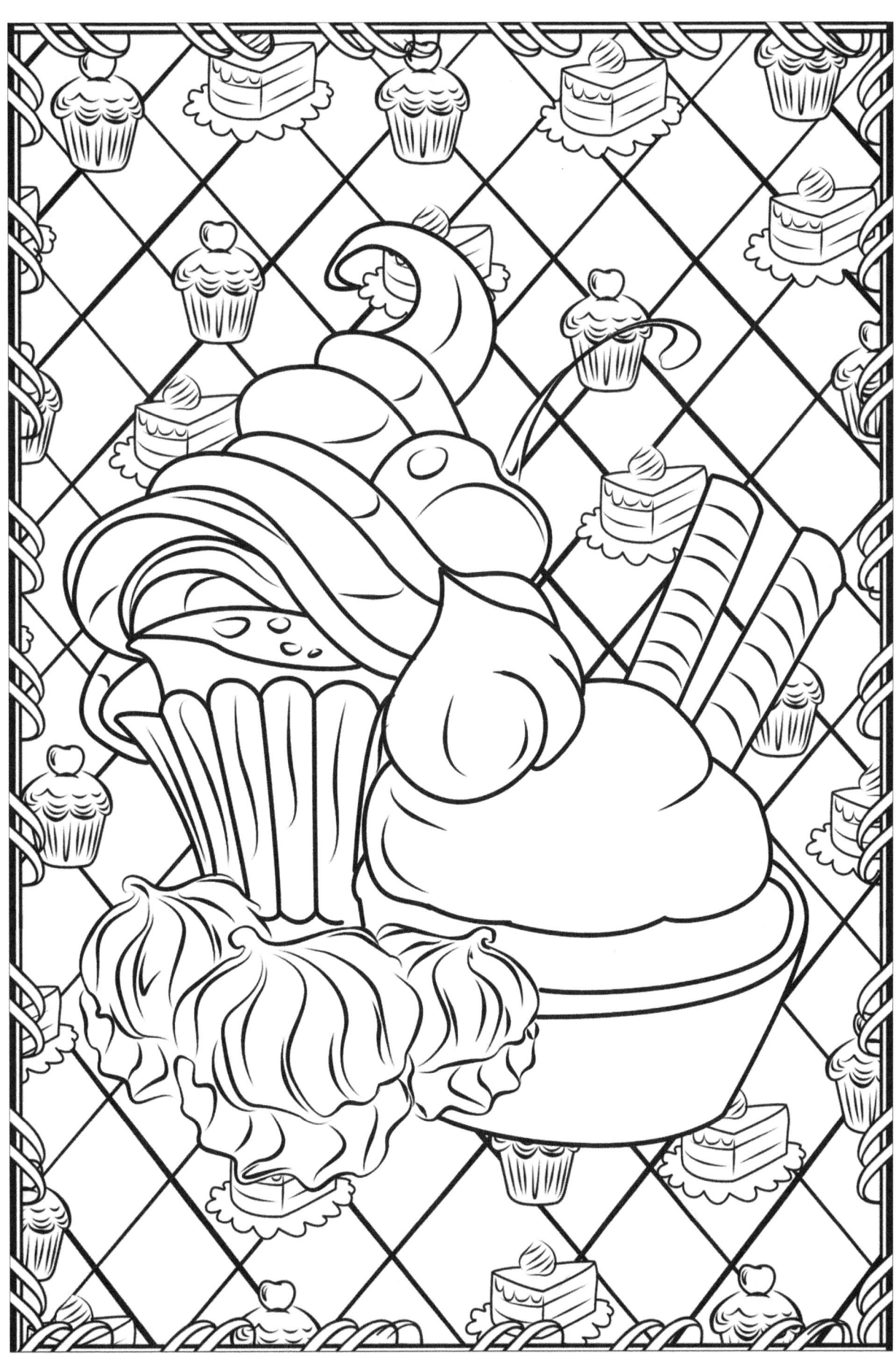

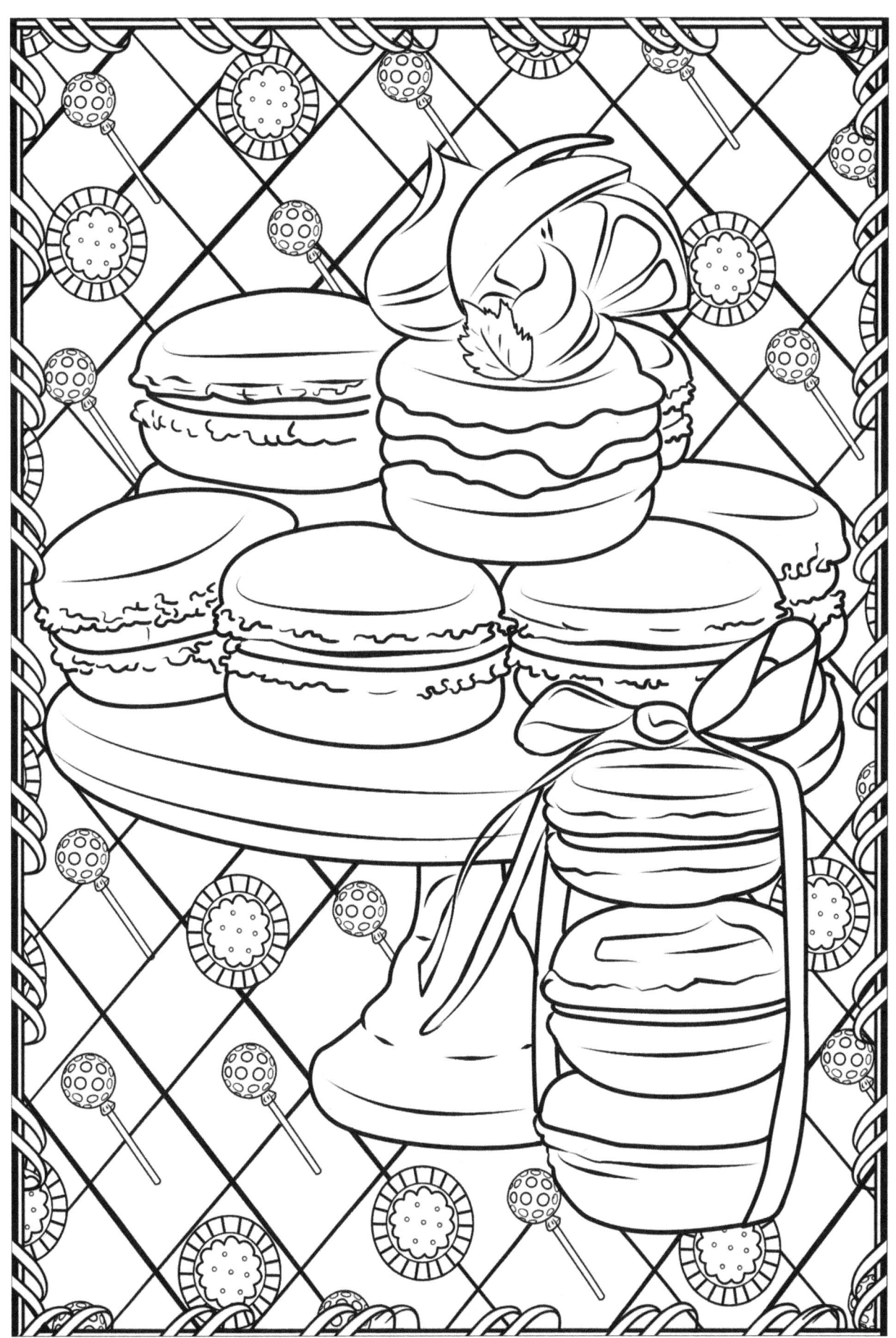

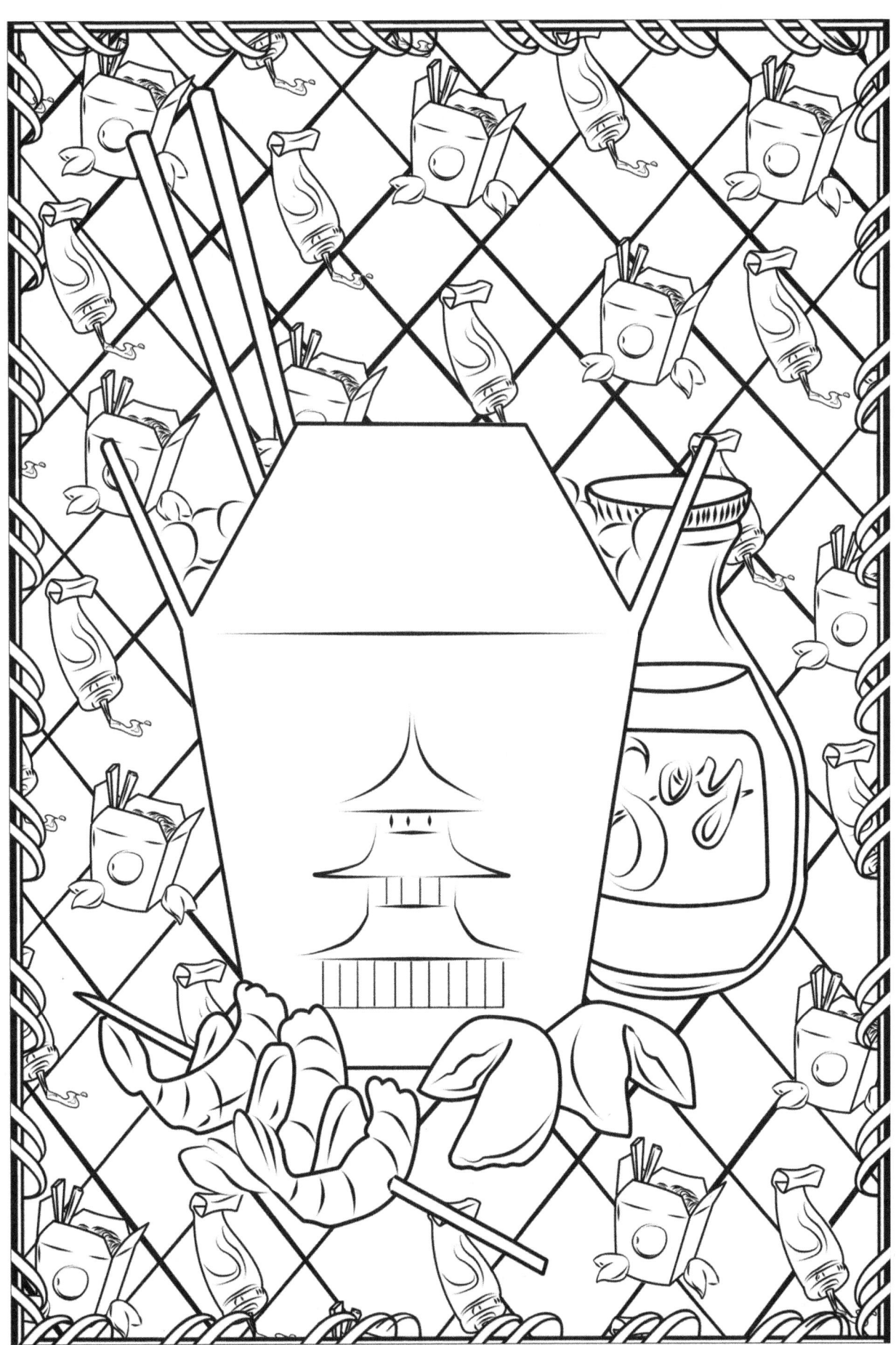

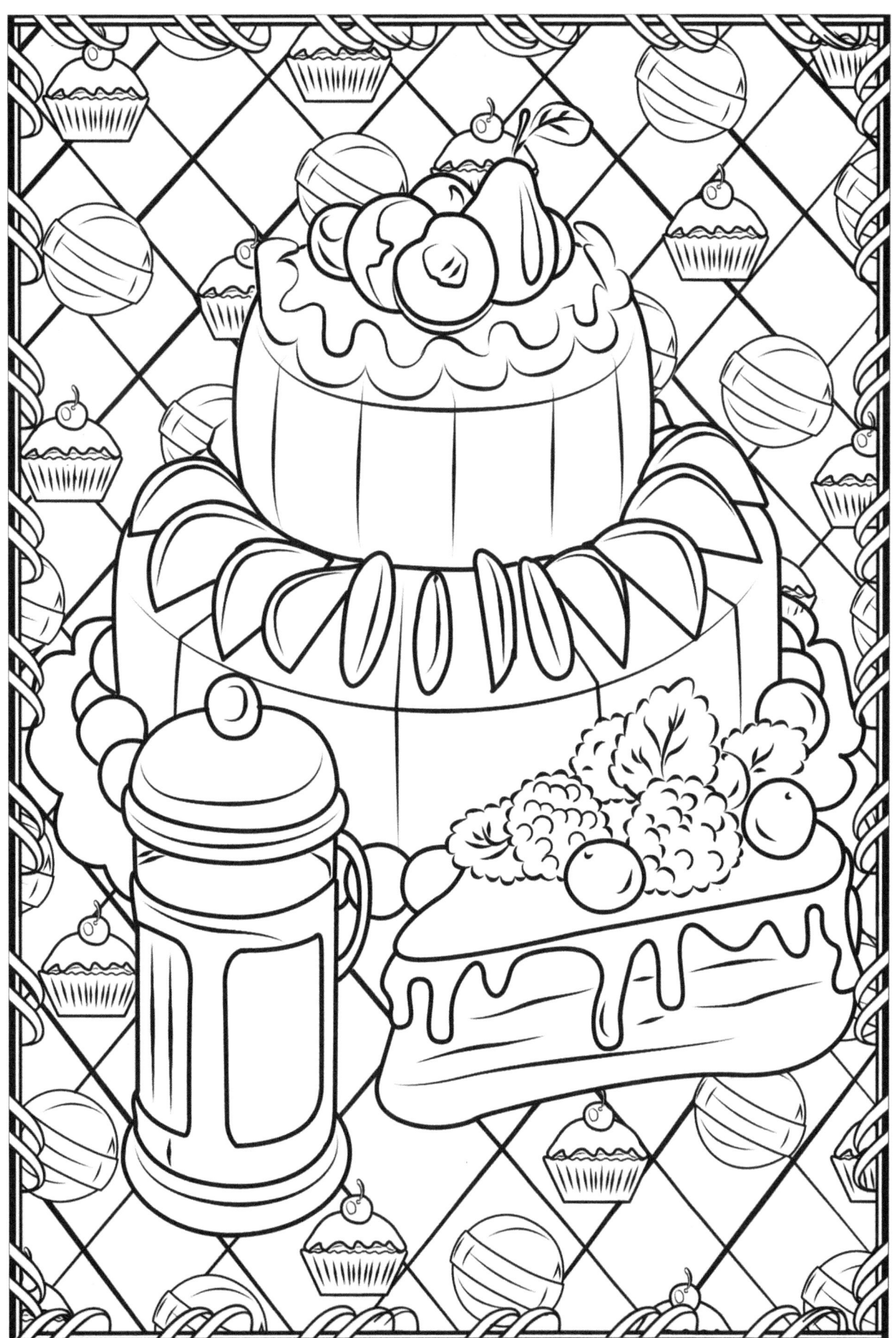

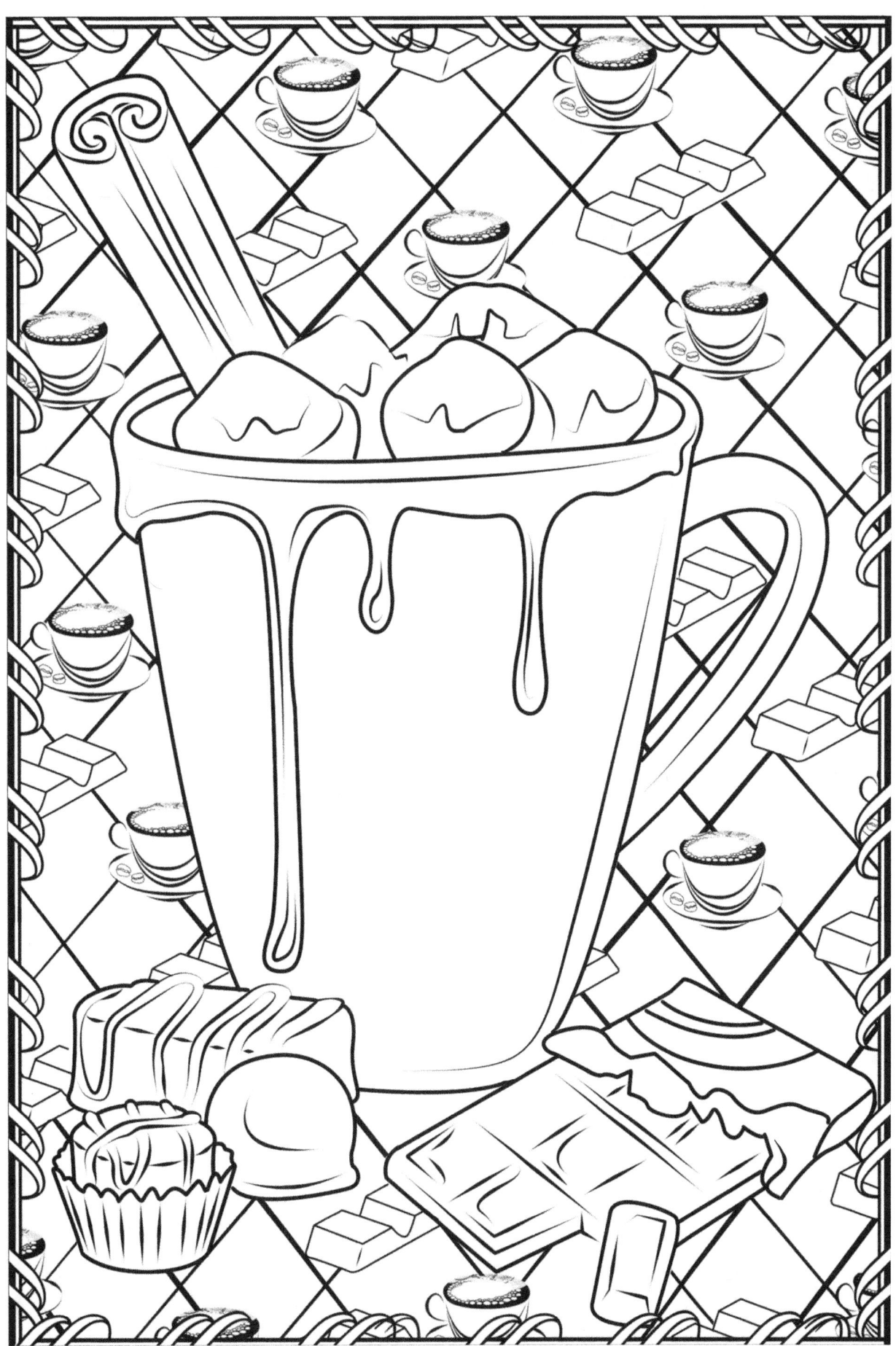

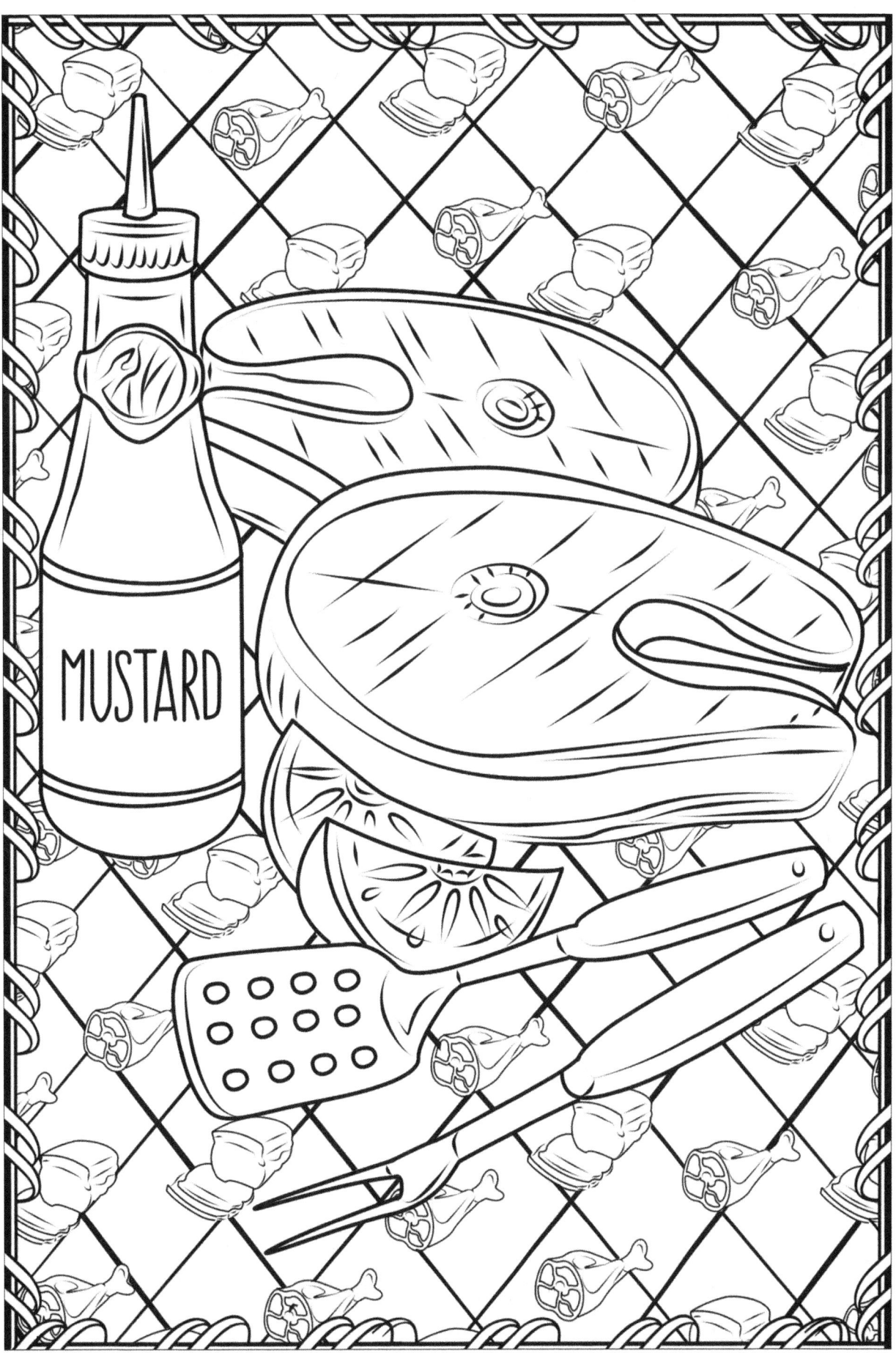

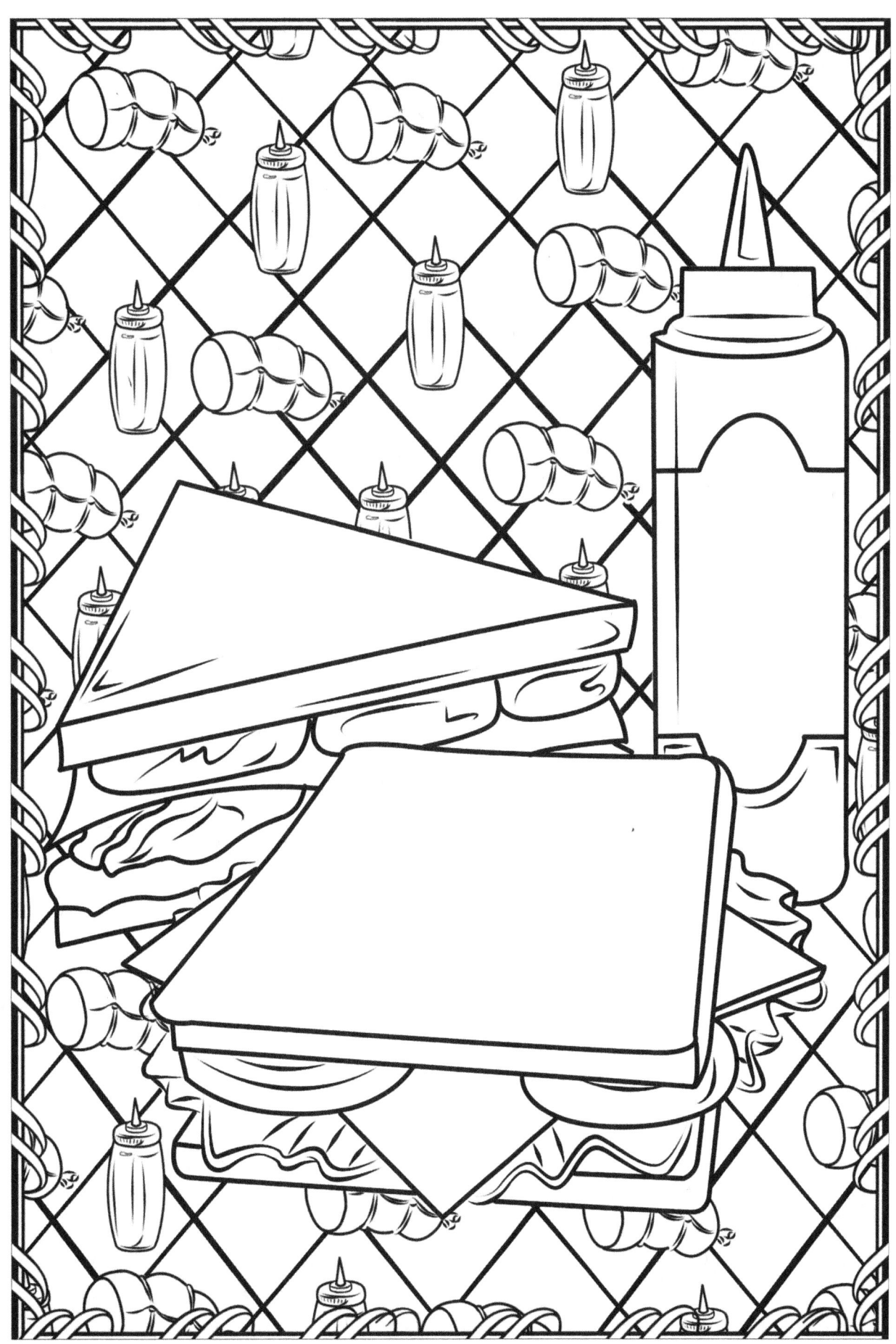

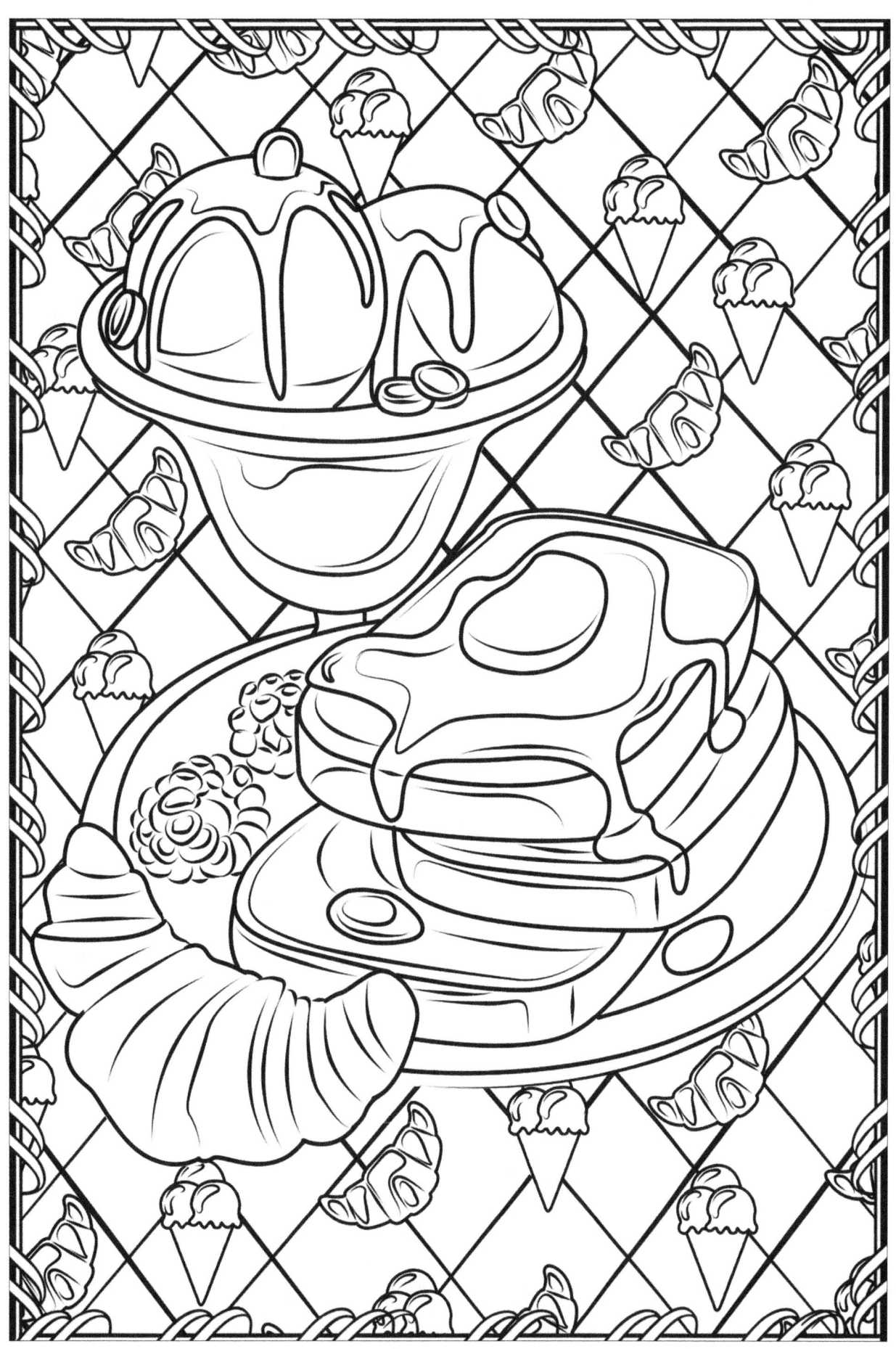

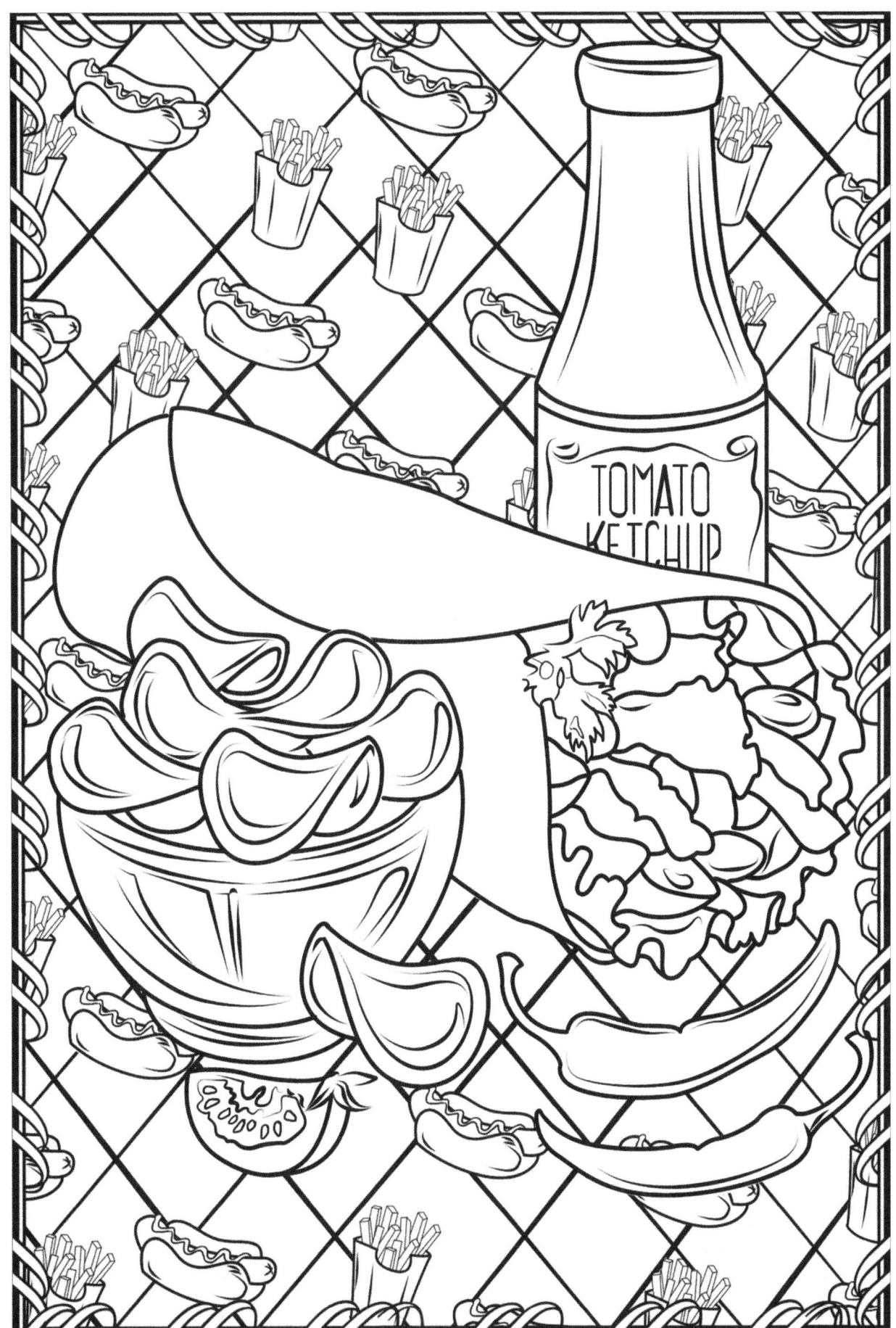

www.ingramcontent.com/pod-product-compliance
Lightning Source LLC
Chambersburg PA
CBHW062223220526
45471CB00009B/3322